THE HIGH SCHOOL STUDENT'S GUIDE TO

Research Papers

101 Ways to Make Your Work Stand Out

Jessica E. Piper

THE HIGH SCHOOL STUDENT'S GUIDE TO RESEARCH PAPERS: 101 WAYS TO MAKE YOUR WORK STAND OUT

*I
808.02
P665*

Copyright © 2017 Atlantic Publishing Group, Inc.

1405 SW 6th Avenue • Ocala, Florida 34471 • Phone 800-814-1132 • Fax 352-622-1875
Website: www.atlantic-pub.com • Email: sales@atlantic-pub.com
SAN Number: 268-1250

Library of Congress Cataloging-in-Publication Data

Names: Piper, Jessica E., 1994- author.
Title: The high school student's guide to research papers : 101 ways to make your work stand out / by Jessica E. Piper.
Description: Ocala, Florida : Atlantic Publishing Group, Inc., [2017] | Includes bibliographical references and index.
Identifiers: LCCN 2017000725 (print) | LCCN 2017010605 (ebook) | ISBN 9781620231876 (alk. paper) | ISBN 1620231875 (alk. paper) | ISBN 9781620231883 (ebook)
Subjects: LCSH: Report writing. | Research. | English language—Composition and exercises—Study and teaching (Secondary)
Classification: LCC LB1047.3 .P56 2017 (print) | LCC LB1047.3 (ebook) | DDC 428.0071/2—dc23
LC record available at https://lccn.loc.gov/2017000725

Printed in the United States

PROJECT MANAGER AND EDITOR: Rebekah Sack
ASSISTANT EDITOR: Cathie Bucci
COVER DESIGN: Jackie Miller
INTERIOR LAYOUT AND JACKET DESIGN: Nicole Sturk

Reduce. Reuse.
RECYCLE.

A decade ago, Atlantic Publishing signed the Green Press Initiative. These guidelines promote environmentally friendly practices, such as using recycled stock and vegetable-based inks, avoiding waste, choosing energy-efficient resources, and promoting a no-pulping policy. We now use 100-percent recycled stock on all our books. The results: in one year, switching to post-consumer recycled stock saved 24 mature trees, 5,000 gallons of water, the equivalent of the total energy used for one home in a year, and the equivalent of the greenhouse gases from one car driven for a year.

Over the years, we have adopted a number of dogs from rescues and shelters. First there was Bear and after he passed, Ginger and Scout. Now, we have Kira, another rescue. They have brought immense joy and love not just into our lives, but into the lives of all who met them.

We want you to know a portion of the profits of this book will be donated in Bear, Ginger and Scout's memory to local animal shelters, parks, conservation organizations, and other individuals and nonprofit organizations in need of assistance.

— Douglas & Sherri Brown,
President & Vice-President of Atlantic Publishing

Table of Contents

Contributors

Laken Brooks is a current Education and Literature student at Emory & Henry College in VA. She has taught English in Brazil and India and has worked to develop curriculum through Harari College Worldwide. She is passionate about equal education and most of her work revolves around how writing and literature can unite students of all backgrounds, helping them find their potential and communicate in a diverse world.

Jen Garcia is a licensed mental health counselor in the state of Massachu-setts. She has lived and worked in Boston, MA and the greater metro area for over a decade. A graduate from Northeastern University with a Master's of Science in Counseling Psychology, Jen is most passionate about her counseling work at a Boston Public High School. There she sees kids who struggle with depression, anxiety and eating disorders as well post-trau-matic stress and attachment disorders. As a double major in English and Psychology as an undergrad she wrote a ridiculous amount of papers. Then in Northeastern University's graduate program she wrote even more! Jen feels she must have done something right because she graduated with a 3.9 GPA (her personal best in all her years of schooling). She is thrilled to put her hard work to good use!

Sarah Seitz is a graduate of Vanderbilt University and double-majored in English and Human and Organizational Development. Over the years, she has taught English to middle and high school students, teaching them how to love the creative, analytical process of writing. She is now the founder of The Enrichery, a comprehensive education company that offers tutoring, college admissions guidance, and summer internship programs.

David D. Timony is assistant professor and Chair of the Education Department at Delaware Valley University in Doylestown, Pennsylvania. Prior to his arrival at DelVal, Dr. Timony taught research and statistics courses in Temple University's Graduate Department of Psychological Studies in Education and worked as a high school learning specialist in Philadelphia where he taught research and study skills. His personal research focuses on the identification, measurement, and development of expertise and high-level skill and has been presented nationally, internationally, and online. When not at his desk, Dr. Timony enjoys spending time with his family and practicing Brazilian Jiu Jitsu.

Jennifer Thomas is a veteran English teacher having taught high school and college-level courses in two different states over the years. She holds a BA in English from Illinois State University, earned her teaching certification at University of Central Florida, and completed graduate research work at the University of Illinois. She enjoys learning from her students every day.

Introduction

The words "research paper" quickly inspire fear among many high schoolers, as if behind each assignment sheet lurks a many-tentacled monster, ready to rear up and bite them. Except instead of arms and legs, this monster fights with thesis statements, MLA style, footnotes, peer-reviewed journal articles, and primary sources.

When facing a research paper, many students struggle to know where to begin. How do you pick a topic that is broad enough to make research relatively painless, but narrow enough that your paper doesn't turn into a book? How do you tell if articles you find on the internet are credible? How do you turn ideas in your head into pretty sentences on the blank, white screen in front of you? This book will answer all of these questions and more.

The 101 tips included in this book don't involve using a big font or wide margins to make your paper seem longer. They do include advice on how to conduct research effectively and efficiently, how to craft an argument based on your own ideas, and how to make your writing sound impressive and professional.

This book also showcases research paper samples, so you can see what thesis statements, revising, footnotes, and other teacher-beloved buzzwords actually look like. And it includes testimony from actual teachers, so you can learn what they expect when they assign a research paper.

Research papers might seem intimidating, but when you pull back the curtain, you'll see that the monster isn't so scary. If you follow the steps described in this book, you'll not only slay the monster, but impress your teacher, create work you are proud of, and learn something along the way.

CHAPTER 1

What is a Research Paper?

So you've been assigned a research paper. Some students want to start right away—if you have to turn in 2,000 words by the end of the month, you may as well start writing now! But soon you find yourself sitting in front of your computer with the cursor ticking and the empty white screen a little too bright. You can't figure out what to write.

Other students choose to wait—it doesn't make sense to start writing a paper until you have good ideas. You might as well give yourself time to think about it.

As is turns out, you need to find a happy medium between both of these approaches. A research paper is a big project, which means you shouldn't try to tackle it without a plan. At the same time, you don't want to leave all your work for the last minute.

Tip · #1 ¶ ▸

Start · working · on · your · research · paper · well · in · advance · of · the · deadline. ¶

A research paper has two critical components, both of which are given in the name. First, you have to do research—you have to investigate on your own using books, the Internet, interviews, experiments, or other methods to learn about a particular topic. After you understand your topic, you can begin to write about it, and turn your knowledge into something that other people can appreciate too.

Research is what makes your research paper different from other academic essays you have written in the past. A research paper expects you to first research your topic, form an argument about your topic, and back that argument up with facts.

"A research paper is a long-term goal. Make sure that you are giving yourself around two weeks, if not more, to plan your paper and research. Some papers require much more in-depth research, especially if it's a longer paper or if it concerns a topic that is more obscure. Many writers sabotage themselves because they underestimate how much time it will take them to actually find useful and reliable sources to use in their papers. My philosophy is to give yourself a week longer than what you think you'll need—you won't be rushed to turn in a last-minute project, and you will have plenty of time to evolve your ideas."

—Laken Brooks, English teacher and curriculum developer

Tip · #2 ¶ ➤

Break · your · research · paper · down · into · chunks · or · stages · that · you · think · you · can · manage. · Then, · set · deadlines · for · each · of · these · stages · to · make · sure · you · don't · fall · behind. ¶

If you're still overwhelmed, you might be wondering if you can avoid research papers altogether. You can't. Research papers are assigned in every subject area. Whether you're studying literature, history, science, politics, philosophy, or even math, you'll likely have to write a research paper at some point. Even if you make it through high school without writing a research paper, you will certainly have to write several in college. Learning to research and write now will make your life easier in the future.

"Self-motivation and self-discipline are some of the hardest skills to develop. I highly recommend creating a schedule for yourself that includes rewards. For example, once you've finished your outline, reward yourself with your favorite snack. Incentivize yourself by scheduling a Netflix and chill date after you've completed your rough draft. Additionally, schedule yourself in such a way that you intentionally leave "buffer" room for mistakes. For example, your paper is due 30 days from now. Aim to have the paper completed by day 27 and you've still given yourself three days in case of emergency."

—Jen Garcia, licensed mental health counselor

Thinking About Research

All research papers involve the same basic process: you collect information, organize your ideas, and write. However, not all research papers are the same, and research papers can serve several different purposes. As you plan your own research paper, it's important to think about what the purpose of your paper is, and how you can conduct your research in the best possible way to accomplish this purpose.

You might think that research is just about getting answers. Of course, at the end of your project you'll need to have them, but the beginning of your research is about asking questions. This section will examine the most frequently assigned types of research papers, and the kinds of questions that will help you begin your research for each one.

Tip · #3 | ¶ ➤
Research · papers · typically · address · complicated · questions — they · do · not · have · simple · yes/no · answers. ¶

Good research is all about planning, so this is a great question. Every good research paper is partially written as part of the research question. Whatever it is that has your interest also has some hypothesis regarding your expectations. It is important to write throughout the process so you do not forget your great ideas later on when the paper is closer to completion. I have found it helpful to give myself a timeline and a writing goal (word count) for each component. The more research you do, the more questions you will have and the more interested you will get—plan well to keep yourself on task!

—David D. Timony, Ph.D.

Identifying cause and effect

Many research papers will ask you to examine how events or ideas impacted one another. This kind of research paper is common in many subjects—your history teacher might ask you to examine a series of historical events; a paper you write for language arts might ask you to determine how a historical event influenced a work of literature; a politics or economics class might ask you to examine how recent events led to a country's current situation.

When you are writing about cause and effect, it is important to have a good understanding of chronology. Chronology refers to the order and timing of events—you can't understand how events impacted each other if you don't know when they happened.

It's important to remember the following principle when you're studying cause and effect: Correlation doesn't necessarily mean causation. Just because two events coincided, or one took place after the other one, doesn't mean the two events are necessarily related. An extreme example: Global pirate attacks have decreased substantially since the 1800s. At the same time, global temperatures have steadily increased since the 1800s. An inexperienced researcher might see these trends and attribute the increase in temperatures to the decrease in pirates—maybe pirates were helping keep the planet cool!

Of course, that's ridiculous. Pirates and global temperatures are unrelated. That is why it is important to consider alternate explanations when you are researching cause and effect. If you think one event might have impacted another, ask yourself: Could this have happened by coincidence? What are other possible explanations for these events?

Some examples of questions or assignments that ask you to analyze cause and effect are:

- What is responsible for the rise in global temperatures in the second half of the 20th century?

- What factors led the United States to use atomic bombs against Japan at the end of World War II?

- To what extent did the collapse of the housing market in the mid-2000s cause the 2008 recession?

Analyzing a work

Some research papers will ask you to analyze specific works of literature, film, or important historical documents. You might be familiar with this sort of research if you've written literary analysis essays before—this type of paper is common in language arts, and also appears in subjects like history or film.

You might think that analyzing a specific document, book, or work of art seems like a narrow topic, but art and literature can tell us a lot about culture and society. Your task is to figure out what the author or creator was saying, or to read or examine a work closely in order to come up with a new idea about how one of its smaller pieces affects your understanding of it as a whole. For example, if your teacher wants you to analyze J.D. Salinger's *The Catcher in the Rye*, you might focus on the effect of the main character's unique and surprising narrative voice.

If your assignment asks you to analyze a particular work, it is important to think about its context. Who created it? What factors influenced the author or creator? What was their audience—who were they writing or speaking for? Are there similar works from this time period?

Here are a few examples of assignment questions that ask you to analyze specific works:

- What does the novel *Crime and Punishment* by Russian author Fyodor Dostoevsky say about the intrusion of Western ideas into Russia during the 1800s?

- What was President Abraham Lincoln's purpose in delivering the Gettysburg Address during the Civil War?

- What does Beyoncé's visual album *Lemonade* say about black women's role in modern American society?

Solving a problem

A research paper might also ask you to solve a specific problem. If you're writing a research paper for a science class, you might have to conduct an experiment or do calculations to determine an outcome. A philosophy paper might ask you to use logic to work through an old paradox.

If your research paper requires you to solve a problem, it's important to plan ahead. You might need data—can you collect it yourself? Do outside sources provide the data you need?

Examples of research paper subjects that ask you to solve a problem:

- How much would it cost to power your hometown with entirely renewable energy?

- What is the best way to prevent teen pregnancy?

- Can we create a mathematical model to predict the weather?

Tip · #4 ¶

While · not · all · research · papers · are · written · to · persuade, · your · research · will · often · force · you · to · take · a · stance · on · a · particular · argument. · You · need · to · back · up · all · of · your · opinions · with · facts. ¶

As You Begin

Let's say you have your research paper subject and are ready to begin. You're starting well ahead of the deadline—you know it will be worse if you procrastinate. You've started brainstorming questions, and you want to begin researching, but you still feel a little unsure. This next section will explain how to begin your research, and how to address any problems that come up along the way.

Asking for help

As you begin your research paper, it is important to make sure that you understand your assignment. Many teachers will give you an assignment sheet or a rubric. Read it! If you have questions, ask your teacher. The worst thing you can do to yourself is to research the wrong subject, which wastes a lot of time and delays progress on your assignment.

Tip · #5 ¶

Make · sure · you · know · the · paper's · requirements · before · you · start · your · research. ¶

There are several important requirements to look for when you are beginning your research paper. Most teachers will tell you the expected length of your paper. Make sure to take note of this—a 500 word paper won't require as much research as a 2,500 word paper, so it's helpful to know which one you will be writing. There can be other requirements too. For example, your teacher might ask you to use at least ten sources.

If you are unsure about the requirements of your paper, it's best to ask your teacher. Even if you are uncomfortable, it's always better to be safe than sorry. Your future self will thank you if you ask for help now.

"You are not a mind reader. (If you are, please come see me; I have some questions.) You cannot know what is expected of you if you do not ask. An airplane pilot does not simply jump in a cockpit and produce a flying plane. While your research paper may not save anyone's life, it sure does have a big effect on yours. Do not jump into the proverbial cockpit and begin pushing buttons and pulling levers. Many people love to be asked to help — it makes them feel good, and it builds into your relationship. Asking for help on a research paper gives you practice in asking for help in the bigger things like, for example, if you end up having to fly a plane someday."

—Jen Garcia, licensed mental health counselor

Tip · #6 ¶ ⬉

While · you · are · working · on · your · research · paper, · try · to · find · time · to · ask · your · teacher · questions · if · you · encounter · problems · along · the · way. · Some · students · think · that · asking · many · questions · makes · them · seem · stupid. · In · reality, · it · shows · your · teacher · or · instructor · that · you · care · about · succeeding. ¶

The research process

Now that you have your subject and know your paper's exact requirements, it's time to start your research. It's easy to get overwhelmed as you begin — if you type your subject into Google, you'll likely find tens of thousands of results in a matter of seconds, and if you go to your local library, you might find several thick books with information related to your topic.

Rather than starting your research by looking for all possible information, it's useful to think about what kind of information you need to look for and what particular topics you need to explore.

Tip · #7 ¶

Before · you · begin · your · research · paper, · make · a · list · of · things · you · already · know · about · the · topic · and · a · list · of · things · you · need · to · learn. ¶

For example, let's say the subject of your research paper is President Lincoln's Gettysburg Address. You know that Lincoln gave the speech after the Battle of Gettysburg during the Civil War, but you don't know much about the battle itself. Your list might look something like this:

Things I already know:	Things I still need to research:
• Lincoln was president during the Civil War. • Lincoln gave the speech after the Battle of Gettysburg.	• How long had the Civil War already been going prior to Gettysburg? • What happened at the Battle of Gettysburg?

Things I already know:	Things I still need to research:
• The Gettysburg Address is a fairly short speech.	• Did Lincoln write the speech himself?

Instead of beginning your research by looking for everything related to the Civil War, look for sources that address your specific questions. This way, your research will be more efficient.

Tip · #8 | ¶

When · you · are · working · on · a · research · paper, · try · to · do · most · of · your · research · before · you · begin · writing · the · actual · paper. ¶

It might be tempting to skip the research step and dive straight into your paper, especially if you feel like you already know a lot about your subject. Resist this temptation. If you begin writing your paper before you've conducted your research, you risk later encountering new information that changes your stance or disproves your arguments. In this case, you must also resist the temptation to include only quotes or paraphrases that seem to support your claim, even though the bulk of your research or sources did not. Ignoring strong evidence against your argument or skewing research to better support a shaky claim is known as "cherry-picking" information.

This chapter has addressed the basics of what makes a research paper and how to approach the different kinds of papers you might encounter. The next two chapters will cover how to choose your topic and conduct your research.

Chapter 2

Planning Your Paper

Planning is an incredibly important part of any research paper. During the planning stages, you pick your topic, organize your research, and decide on a thesis statement based on that research. These are important steps—you don't want to skip them.

Think of writing a research paper as setting off on a cross-ocean voyage. During the planning, you create your maps, gather all your supplies, and prepare your boat for send-off. If you miss any of these steps, you are likely to end up lost at sea. Likewise, failure to adequately prepare for your research paper means you will encounter problems later.

Choosing Your Topic

Sometimes your teacher will assign you a specific research topic. Other times, you will choose your own research topic. Picking your own topic can be fun—you get to choose something that is interesting to you. However, there are some risks when you pick your own topic.

> Most of the worst papers that I have read involve a student replacing facts with his or her own opinions, whether or not those opinions are historical truth. In a religion class, I once read a paper arguing that Jesus wrote the Ten Commandments. The student replied: "This is what I was taught in Sunday School, so you cannot tell me that I am wrong. It is what I believe." While every person is certainly entitled to certain personal beliefs, research papers are rooted in fact and must be supported with evidence.
>
> —Laken Brooks, English teacher and curriculum developer

The most common mistake students make when picking a research paper topic is choosing one that is the wrong size. If you choose a topic that is too broad, you will be overwhelmed with information. At the same time, if you pick a topic that is too narrow, you might not be able to find enough information about it.

Tip · #9| ¶ ➤

Pick · a · topic · that · is · neither · too · broad · nor · to · narrow · for · your · assignment. ¶

When picking your research topic, it's important to continue to consider the requirements of the paper. A 500-word paper, for example, requires a more specific topic than a 2,500-word paper.

Narrowing a broad topic

Let's say you're supposed to write a 1,000-word paper for your history class. You can write about any subject you want, and you've chosen to write about World War II, because you think it's really interesting.

Many historians have written 1,000-page books on World War II—you shouldn't try to write a 1,000-word paper about it. The first thing you can do to narrow your topic is ask yourself: What is interesting to me about this subject?

You decide that you're most interested in World War II battles—you've always been interested in military strategy and warfare. But even the topic of World War II battles is pretty broad: The war was fought in Europe, the Pacific Ocean, and North Africa. You decide it would be fun to study North Africa, because you've never learned about that part of the war before.

Since you don't know a lot about North Africa during World War II, you can run a quick internet search to see what you discover. The second result is a news article from a series telling the story of World War II in retrospective. You read the first paragraph, which gives an overview of how the Allies fought back to ultimately defeat the Axis Powers in 1943.

You decide to write your paper on how the Allied forces won the North African campaign during World War II. That's much narrower topic, and it's much better for a 1000-word paper.

Broadening a narrow topic

Some students have the opposite problem. They pick a topic so specific it is very difficult to research. For example, let's say you have been assigned a 1,000-word paper about history. You like to go running in the woods behind your backyard, so you decide to research the history of nature preservation in your town.

When you start doing your research, however, you run into problems. There haven't been any books written about your subject. You make a few phone calls—maybe you can find someone to interview—but no one in your town seems to have the information you are looking for.

In this case, you should broaden your topic. If you're really interested in nature preservation, you could research the history of nature preservation in the United States, as there are lots of books about Teddy Roosevelt's efforts to establish national parks. Or, if you want your project to be more grounded in local history, you can examine the natural history of your state or region, instead of just your town.

Organizing Your Research

It's important to be organized when you are conducting your research. You might be able to form a thesis statement based on your general impressions when you are reading, but you'll need specific quotes, statistics, and examples for the body of your paper. This next section discusses how to organize your notes and research.

Taking good notes

There's a frustrating feeling you get when you're sitting in front of your computer writing a draft of your paper, and you can't remember a particular fact. Maybe it's a statistic—was it 13 percent or 31? Maybe it's a quote—you remember reading something really powerful that an American soldier said while he was stationed in North Africa in 1942, but you can't remember where you read it.

Tip · #10 ⁊ ➤

Write · down · important · information · in · your · notes—don't · count · on · yourself · to · remember · everything!⁊

You can avoid many problems if you take good notes while you are re searching. Taking research notes is different than taking notes in class. You're probably used to taking notes while your teacher talks, but your re-search notes require you to think about information from many different sources. You'll need to adjust your note-taking strategies.

One way to organize your research is by dividing your topic into smaller categories. Pick a mechanism for keeping track of each category, and sort all of your information accordingly. For example, some people like to use colored note cards to keep track of research. They might have four colors of note cards for their four categories. When they find a new fact, they write it on a notecard of the corresponding color.

Tip · #11 | ¶ ➤
Sort · your · information · within · your · notes. ¶

Many students like to take notes or keep track of information on their computers. That's OK too. You can consider sorting your information using different documents, different colored fonts, or another system that works best for you.

For example, let's say you're writing about Lincoln's Gettysburg Address. First, your paper will consider the historical context for the Gettysburg Address, especially the early Civil War battles. Then, your paper will delve into Lincoln's personal context—his beliefs about slavery and how they evolved over the course of the war. Finally, your paper will analyze the text of the speech itself and interpret Lincoln's words. This arrangement gives you three categories.

Tip · #12 ¶

Make · sure · to · keep · track · of · where · your · information · comes · from. · Knowing · which · sources · provided · you · with · which · material · will · be · important · when · it · is · time · for · citations, · and · it · makes · it · easier · for · you · to · go · back · and · look · up · facts · later. ¶

When you are sorting information into categories, make sure you still know the information's original source. If the information comes from a book, write down the title of the book, the author, and the page number. If it comes from the internet, write down the URL address. If it comes from a different source (a documentary, an interview, or something else), make sure you write enough notes that you can later figure out where the information came from.

Keeping track of where your information comes from makes it easier for you to check your facts later, and it helps ensure you avoid plagiarism, which will be discussed in greater depth in Chapter 4.

The Thesis Statement

You might have heard the term "thesis statement" before. The thesis statement outlines your main point to your reader. It's a big deal!

Tip · #13 ⁋ ➤

Your · thesis · statement · should · state · your · paper's · main · point. ⁋

In a research paper, your thesis statement should be your central argument that you support with facts from your research. This means you have to know quite a bit about your topic before you write your thesis statement. You can't expect to know your own argument before you've done your research.

At the same time, it's helpful to have a general idea of what your thesis will be when you start doing your research. This way, you know which information will be helpful for your paper. Try to come up with a thesis statement fairly early in your research. You can modify it later on if you discover new information.

Tip · #14 ⁋ ➤

Your · thesis · statement · is · the · most · important · part · of · your · research · paper. · It · should · appear · early · in · the · paper, · since · the · rest · of · it · is · all · about · supporting · your · thesis. · You · should · write · your · thesis · statement · before · you · write · the · rest · of · your · paper. ⁋

Your thesis statement is the key to making the strongest paper. A great research paper grade oftentimes comes from two things: interesting and innovative analysis, and correct grammar. Most writers can obey basic grammar rules to write a paper. A quality thesis statement that makes the reader question his or her own stance on an issue is a ticket to a good grade. Even if you include a few misplaced commas or dangling modifiers, your teacher will appreciate your brilliant analysis or argument. This appreciation will oftentimes be reflected in your final grade.

—Laken Brooks, English teacher and curriculum developer

Thesis statement formulas

Your thesis statement is the most important part of your paper. That might sound like a lot of pressure, but the good news is that your thesis statement will be short —most are no longer than two sentences.

Tip · #15

Your · thesis · statement · should · be · one · or · two · sentences.

Most thesis statements fit into two basic formulas. The first formula is known as, "This is true for these reasons." You state your main point and describe, in a very general way, the reasons why that main point is true. The second formula for a thesis statement can be summarized as, "Despite this opposing viewpoint, these reasons are why this is true." This formula allows you to acknowledge other arguments, but explains why your argument is the best.

You'll notice that "this is true" is a part of both thesis statement formulas. The true assertion in your thesis statement shouldn't be any old fact. It should contain your original ideas about your topic, which you developed in the research process.

Your thesis statement should use formal language. You want to sound professional. However, don't go crazy with a thesaurus because you're trying to sound smart. Never use a word in your thesis statement (or anywhere else in your paper) if you don't know what it means.

Tip · #16

Use · strong · words · in · your · thesis · statement · to · make · yourself · sound · credible. · Many · students · are · tempted · to · start · their · thesis · statement · with · the · words · "I · think" · or · "I · believe." · Don't · do · this. · Not · only · is · it · unnecessary, · but · it · makes · you · sound · uncertain.

Your thesis is the promise to your reader for content and structure. It should clearly state the topic, your angle on the topic, and keywords from your outline.

—Jennifer Thomas, veteran English teacher

Example thesis statements

Let's take a look at a couple of our sample topics from Chapter 1 and develop thesis statements for each of them.

Example research topic: What is responsible for the rise in global temperatures in the second half of the 20th century?

> Beginning thesis statement: Temperatures have risen across the globe since the 1950s for reasons that I will explain.

This thesis statement isn't awful. It tells the reader that your paper will be addressing the global rise in temperature. While it says you have reasons to support this claim, it doesn't say what those reasons are. The use of first person (the phrase "I will explain") sounds a bit unprofessional. More importantly, this thesis statement doesn't reflect your own original ideas. Unless you've been taking temperature measurements yourself since the 1950s, this thesis statement is just stating evidence that someone else has collected.

> Revised thesis statement: Temperatures have risen across the globe since the 1950s due to human activities.

This thesis statement is better. It tells the reader your main argument—that human activities have caused an increase in global temperatures since the 1950s. However, it could benefit from more detail.

> Final thesis statement: Although some people claim otherwise, the global increase in temperatures since the 1950s has occurred largely due to human activities, especially the burning of fossil fuels.

This final thesis statement acknowledges that there are perspectives other than your own, but states your main point and provides a hint at the evidence you will use to demonstrate your argument.

Example research topic: What was President Abraham Lincoln's purpose in delivering the Gettysburg Address during the Civil War?

Beginning thesis statement: President Lincoln delivered the Gettysburg Address after the Battle of Gettysburg, which was a really bad battle.

This thesis statement is a starting point. It identifies the subject of the paper, but it doesn't provide any analysis. Lincoln delivering the Gettysburg address is a fact, and your thesis statement should be your own argument. Additionally, the phrase "a really bad battle" is informal and seems out of place.

Revised thesis statement: President Lincoln delivered the Gettysburg Address following the horrific Battle of Gettysburg in order to redefine the American Civil War as not only a conflict between sides, but a struggle for justice.

This thesis statement is much better. It brings in your analysis of why Lincoln delivered the Gettysburg Address.

Final thesis statement: President Lincoln delivered the Gettysburg Address following the horrific Battle of Gettysburg in order to redefine the Civil War as not only a conflict between sides, but a struggle for justice. Lincoln's commitment to human equality can be seen through his allusions to America's founding principles, as outlined in the Declaration of Independence.

This final thesis statement provides even more detail. Not only does it demonstrate your own analysis for why Lincoln delivered the Gettysburg address, but it hints at the evidence you will use to prove your point later in your paper.

Preparing Your Ideas

> # Tip · #17 | ¶ ➤
>
> Do · some · sort · of · brainstorming · or · outlining · before · you · begin · writing · your · paper. · It · might · seem · unnecessary, · but · it · will · make · your · paper · better · and · save · you · time · in · the · long · run. ¶

Brainstorming

Now that you have gathered information and decided on the point you're going to make with it, the next step is translating all this information from separate facts in your notes to a cohesive research paper. Brainstorming is a useful way to draw connections between your ideas and get yourself ready to write. If you've been having trouble drawing a conclusion from your research in order to form a thesis statement, the connections you make between ideas while brainstorming might clarify your main point for you.

Freewriting

One brainstorming technique is known as freewriting. With freewriting, you give yourself a particular amount of time to write down whatever comes to mind about your topic. Because you are writing, you will naturally try to convert your ideas into some sort of narrative, and you might think of things while you are writing that will help with your paper.

You can do a freewrite either by hand or on your computer. When you are freewriting, don't worry about spelling or grammar. Just think about your ideas.

The following is a sample freewrite, continuing with the Gettysburg Address topic:

> Lincoln gave the Gettysburg address after the battle of Gettysburg, which was a really bad battle in the middle of the civil war. It last three days and a lot of people died, so Lincoln came to speak because the Union won and he was the president of the Union. (But he didn't speak right away, it was actually four months after the battle when they were dedicating a monument). His speech was really short and he referenced the founding fathers and freedom a lot. But historians have studied his speech a ton and think it's one of the best speeches ever, so now I'm writing a paper about it.

Mind-mapping

Mind-mapping is another useful brainstorming technique. Mind-mapping lets you draw connections between subjects visually. If you're artistic, you can even break out your colored pencils or rulers. For a mind map, start with your general topic area in the middle of your paper, and branch out, connecting other topics as you go. Don't hold back—exercises like mind-mapping work best when you just let the ideas flow and connect.

The following is a sample mind-map about the Gettysburg Address:

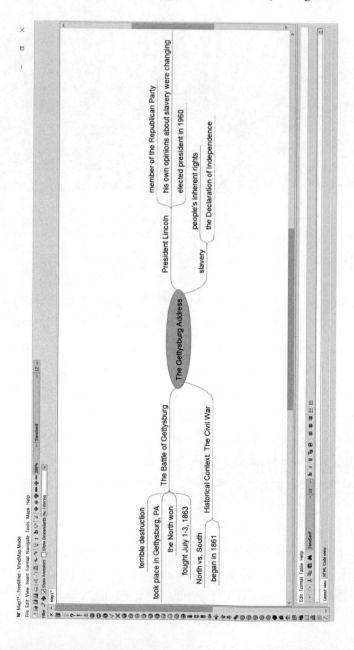

If you prefer to use your computer, you can still create a mind map digitally; there are many online programs that you can use. Check out sites like MindMup (**www.mindmup.com**) and Free Mind (**http://freemind. sourceforge.net**).

> Drafting is essential. Without it, you're doomed to have a disorganized paper. I am a big believer in starting off with a Bubble Map that can show you how your ideas are all related to your one big argument. The thesis bubble goes at the center, and your supporting evidence (quotes/research) are all bubbles that stem from the thesis. Once you've got your map, start a draft. On your draft, begin with your thesis (since everything must always return to the thesis). Then, type out your quotes/research. Then, write a few sentences of analysis after your quotes (explain why the quote proves the thesis). Next, go back and write your topic sentences by asking yourself, "What does this paragraph try to prove?" Then, start filling in whatever is left over.
>
> —Sarah Seitz, Founder of "The Enrichery,"
> a comprehensive education company

Outlining

The most common brainstorming and organization technique is outlining. When outlining, you draft a condensed, bullet-pointed version of your paper that establishes your main ideas and the order they might go in. Your outline might start with your thesis statement and include a few bullet points for each of your main subjects.

The following is an example outline about the Gettysburg Address:

Thesis Statement: President Lincoln delivered the Gettysburg Address following the horrific Battle of Gettysburg in order to redefine the Civil War as not only a conflict between sides, but a struggle for justice. Lincoln's commitment to human equality can be seen through his allusions to America's founding principles, as outlined in the Declaration of Independence.

1. The Battle of Gettysburg was a really horrible conflict in the midst of a really horrible war.

- high casualties
- the battle lasted 3 days

2. Lincoln talks about the founding fathers and the idea of freedom.

- "four score and seven years ago" = 87 years, when the Declaration of Independence was signed
- "a new birth of freedom"

3. Lincoln wanted to redefine the Civil War as a battle for justice and equality.

- Lincoln's own views on slavery were changing
- making slavery a moral issue might inspire people and help the North win the war

When you are going to take a trip, you make a plan. You decide what you are going to do, where you are going to go, etc. etc. Writing a research paper is like going on a trip: you can avoid a lot of trouble and confusion when you start with a plan. Typically, you can begin by brainstorming. Brainstorming doesn't have to be structured or even in complete sentences. When you have your ideas and sources, you can move to outlining. Outlining helps you begin physically forming your paper, deciding on the topic of each paragraph.

After outlining, you can move to your first draft. Your first draft, or rough draft, does not need to be perfect but it does need to involve most, if not all, of your sources and be written in a grammatically correct, ordered fashion. I suggest that you take a break after writing your first draft. When we leave our papers alone for a week or so and then come back to them to read them at a later date, we can oftentimes find more mistakes than when we first wrote it. In the meantime, consider sending your first draft to a friend, teacher, or tutor to look over your paper and give you suggestions. The revision process involves working with a well-formed draft and doing some basic reorganization, double-checking your spelling and punctuation, and pruning it to be the best it can be. In this process, perhaps your paper is nearly complete and all you need to do to make it perfect is to insert another quotation or remove a paragraph.

—Laken Brooks, English teacher and curriculum developer

Brainstorming is an essential part of the research paper process. You don't have to try every brainstorming activity, but it's a good idea to try something. You can also mix and match—create a mind map or freewrite to get yourself thinking, and then make an outline once your ideas are more developed.

Once you've brainstormed, you can begin writing your paper. Instead of sitting in front of the computer, unsure of what to say, you already have your ideas ready. You are setting off for your voyage prepared with maps, supplies, and a sturdy boat. It should be a good journey.

Chapter 3

Conducting Research

The first chapter of this book discussed what makes a research paper different from other assignments you've done before. You have to support your claims with facts and information. Of course, you're not expected to know all the facts about a topic for a research paper—you're a student, not a walking encyclopedia.

Before you write your paper, you have to conduct research yourself. This means you have to find sources related to your topic and read or examine them. Researching for a major paper might seem like a scary proposition, but chances are it is something you have done before. If you've ever looked up something on the Internet or read a nonfiction book to learn something, you've already conducted research. In fact, you are conducting research by reading this book about research papers!

Your research paper will require you to conduct rigorous research in a particular subject area. This chapter is devoted to exploring the many ways that you can research. It will also discuss some of the common mistakes students make when researching and how to avoid them.

You'll learn how to find sources on the Internet, in books, and in places you probably wouldn't expect. You'll read about databases and libraries, and you'll hear a little more about encyclopedias, but thankfully, you won't encounter any walking ones.

What Counts as a Source?

You are probably familiar with reading books and using the Internet, and this chapter will later discuss how to find the best print and electronic sources. But online articles and library books aren't the only sources you can use for your research paper.

Tip · #18 ❡ ➤

Don't · limit · yourself · by · only · using · sources · that · you · can · read. · Documentaries, · photos, · the · radio, · and · podcasts · can · be · useful · sources · as · well. ❡

For example, documentaries can be a great source for your research papers. Often, you can find documentaries at a library, and many documentaries even end up on sites like YouTube—look around and see what you can find. If you do watch a documentary on YouTube, make sure it includes the name of the filmmaker or director and when it was made so that you can cite it.

> "Your college library should offer some memberships to online scholarly journals and search engines. Yes, librarians still exist—and you can ask them for help! Most of the online journals available will contain pieces that qualify as scholarly articles."
>
> —Jen Garcia, licensed mental health counselor

Nearly anything can be a source for your paper, but not all sources are good. The next few sections will address different kinds of sources, and how to determine the reliability of each one.

Tip · #19 ¶

Depending · on · your · subject area, · you · might · be · able · to · conduct · interviews · for · your · research · paper. · If · you · live · near · a · college · or · university, · see · if · there · is · a · professor · who · is · an · expert · on · your · topic. · Even · if · the · professor · you · contact · isn't · an · expert · on · your · specific · topic, · it · is · likely · they · will · be · able · to · point · you · towards · the · right · person · or · source. · If · you · are · writing · about · historical · events · that · happened · in · the · last · 75 · years, · see · if · you · can · find · someone · still · alive · who · might · have · been · a · witness. ¶

Primary, secondary, and tertiary sources

There are three kinds of sources: primary, secondary, and tertiary. Of these three types, tertiary sources are the most general. Tertiary sources refer to encyclopedias, atlases, or other reference books that you might use at the very beginning of your research. These sources might provide you with basic background information, help you come up with keywords for further research, or direct you to other sources. Because they provide such basic information, tertiary sources should not make up the bulk of your research.

> # Tip · #20| ¶ ⬉
>
> Tertiary · sources, · such · as · encyclopedias, · are · a · good · way · to · introduce · yourself · to · a · topic · that · you · don't · know · very · well. ¶

Secondary sources are sources written by other researchers who have studied the same topic as you. Textbooks, biographies, and journal articles are a few examples of secondary sources. People who write secondary sources typically write them by examining primary and other secondary sources.

Primary sources are firsthand accounts of information without additional interpretation. They include raw research data from experiments, original works of fiction, statistics, interviews, letters, diaries, photographs, eyewitness accounts, and many government records. Don't use a work of fiction as a primary source unless you're writing about that work, its genre, or its creator. For example, Steven Spielberg's movie *Lincoln* is not a credible source for your paper about Abraham Lincoln and the Gettysburg Address.

It is, however, a credible source for a paper about Steven Spielberg's film techniques.

> # Tip · #21 ¶ ➤
>
> Many · primary · sources, · such · as · old · photographs · or · newspaper · clippings, · are · now · digitized · and · available · online. · The · Library · of · Congress · (loc.gov) · and · the · National · Archives · (archives.gov) · are · good · places · to · start · looking · for · primary · sources · pertaining · to · American · history. ¶

Evaluating sources

If you conduct enough research, you'll notice that your sources will sometimes contradict one another. For example, some sources say that there were 28,000 Confederate casualties at the Battle of Gettysburg, while others say that there were only 23,000.

Sometimes two sources might use the same facts, but present them in very different ways. Or sources may cherry-pick information and intentionally leave out certain facts that contradict their point. It is your job as a researcher to be on the lookout for misleading sources and to conduct enough research that you don't repeat their conclusions.

Fact-checking

Fact-checking is a key component of research. As a general rule, it is always better if you can find the same information in multiple sources.

Tip · #22 | ¶ ▶

Double-check · important · facts · with · multiple · sources. · If · many · sources · give · you · the · same · information, · it · is · more · likely · that · the · information · is · true · than · it · would · be · if · you · only · found · the · information · in · one · source. ¶

Sometimes you will realize that even the experts don't have an exact answer to a particular issue. For example, historians really don't know how many Confederate soldiers were killed during the Battle of Gettysburg. If you were writing a paper about the Gettysburg Address and wanted to include this fact, you might just say that between 23,000 and 28,000 soldiers were killed, according to historical estimates. It is OK to acknowledge the limitations of your research.

Tip · #23 ⁋ ⬉

Some · articles · and · journals · are · peer-reviewed, · which · means · a · team · of · experts · examined · the · articles · and · helped · revise · them. · These · are · good · sources. ⁋

Sometimes, experts have already done fact-checking for you. Peer-reviewed journal articles refer to academic papers, often written by college and graduate school professors. These papers undergo thorough editing and fact-checking by other researchers before they are published. Look for peer-reviewed articles — they are reliable.

Your source is probably reputable if it is published in a peer-reviewed journal. University research will most likely be more reputable than a local newspaper. Another simple test is to ask yourself why the source wrote their article or book. Is it to gain publicity or sell a product? Is it to elect a politician or promote a specific religion, charity, or organization? If you answer "yes" to these questions, your source is probably biased and not reputable.

—Laken Brooks, English teacher and curriculum developer

Tip · #24 ⁋ ⬉

Check · the · date · of · your · sources · when · you · fact-check · them. ⁋

When you are fact-checking, you should also always check the date of your sources. Science and technology, for example, have made a lot of progress in recent years. If you are looking at a scientific paper from many years ago, you might want to see if there are more recent papers that support or contradict that one.

Bias

Bias refers to an author's tendency to promote a particular point of view. A source might be biased if the author intentionally misleads the reader or omits key information in order to make a point. But bias doesn't have to be malicious—some authors are biased simply because of their experience of the world.

Tip · #25 ⁋

Even · if · sources · are · factually · correct, · they · can · still · exhibit · bias. ⁋

Author credibility and bias

To determine if a source exhibits bias, you can start by learning about its author. Look for the author's credentials. Are they an expert in their field? Do they have fancy titles or degrees, and are these relevant? For example, if you are reading a book on the Civil War, an author who is a history professor at a college or university would be credible. An author with a Ph.D. in math might be a very smart person, but a less credible historian.

When you are investigating a source's author, also consider what associations or affiliations the author might have. For example, if an author who is writing about the connection between fossil fuels and climate change is also employed by an oil company, their job might pose a conflict of interest and cause bias in their work.

Your evaluation of a source's reliability and bias shouldn't be based on the author alone. Someone without formal education can still conduct good research—that's why it's a good idea to examine what (if any) sources an author cites. If an author has acquired their information from reliable sources, they are likely to have created a reliable source too.

Over the course of your research, you'll likely find anonymous sources—sources with no author listed. Generally, try to avoid these. If there is no author, no one is accountable for whether the information is correct.

Bias words

Regardless of the author of a source, you should evaluate the source yourself for bias. Certain keywords can tip you off that a source might be exhibiting substantial bias.

Watch out for vague or non-specific language, as it allows authors to argue weak claims without being "technically" wrong. For example, the word "many" can be meaningless in a research paper. If the author says "many people" believe something, they could mean that 10 people believe it, or 50, or 500,000. Authors might use language like this when they really have no idea what the actual number is—don't be fooled! Likewise, be wary of authors who say "studies show" or "the data indicate" without listing any studies or data to back up their claims.

Finally, watch out for authors who use strong or loaded language. Trust your instincts—if the tone of a piece seems angry, or overly positive, or overtly leaning to one side, it's probably biased.

When is bias OK?

When you conduct your research, you'll find that many sources have bias. When you discover that a source is biased, you don't necessarily have to throw it out. As the researcher, you have to account for their bias, either by discounting certain facts or studying other sources with different biases until you get a complete picture.

Tip · #26 ¶ ➤

A · source · can · have · bias · but · still · be · useful. · Biased · primary · sources · might · explain · an · individual's · motivations · or · intentions. · Make · sure · that · you · remain · an · objective · researcher · and · you · consider · the · source's · bias · when · you · are · writing · your · paper.¶

Primary sources are very likely to exhibit bias. For example, if you are researching history, you might stumble across old diaries or letters belonging to historic figures. These sources can be incredibly valuable, but they will almost certainly contain bias, as they were not written to be objective. Your job is to ensure that you don't pick up the tendencies and inclinations of your sources — your final research paper should be an unbiased source.

Go to the Library

Although it's possible to find sources online, it's good to start your research at a library. Libraries have encyclopedias and reference books to help you gather background information. They likely have books specific to your topic, and librarians who are trained to help you with your research.

Tip · #27

Librarians · at · your · school · or · public · library · know · a · lot · about · finding · print · and · electronic · sources. · If · you · can't · find · a · source · you · are · looking · for, · ask · for · help.

Libraries often have another important tool — access to archives and databases. Many libraries allow you to look through old newspaper articles on microfilm. Libraries often subscribe to journals and magazines, and have copies going back many years. Although some students think they can find everything on the Internet, that's simply not true. Don't limit yourself and your research by sticking close to your computer.

Tip · #28

Schools · and · libraries · often · have · online · databases · that · you · cannot · get · at · home. · Ask · your · teacher · or · librarian · about · accessing · online · databases.

> Believe it or not, the library is the best starting point. Librarians are well-equipped with a broad range of options to put you on the right track to quality sources in hard copy and mobile formats. Modern libraries are equipped with remote login capabilities and are prepared to orient students on the best uses of all online research sites.
>
> —David D. Timony, Ph.D.

Books, books, books!

The internet may be a more popular form of research now, but books are an incredibly important resource. Unlike Internet sources, books typically undergo a thorough editing and fact-checking process, so they are likely to be reliable.

Tip · #29 ¶

Reading · several · books · on · your · subject · matter · can · be · daunting, · especially · if · you · are · busy. · Use · the · Table · of · Contents · in · a · book · to · figure · out · which · parts · will · be · most · relevant · for · you, · and · read · those · first. ¶

Some students are overwhelmed by books—it's much easier to read a two-page article than a 250-page book. However, a book is likely to have much more information than a single article. If you only read short articles about your topic, you might miss out on the bigger picture. Books are likely to tell a complete story or narrative.

Let's say you are supposed to write a research paper on the Civil War. If you find a book on the Civil War, the author of that book has already done a lot of the research that you are trying to do. Reading their book isn't really a terrible burden — it's a shortcut to gaining a lot of knowledge.

Tip · #30 ⸿ ➤

Most · books · have · extensive · bibliographies — lists · of · the · sources · that · the · authors · used · when · writing · the · book. · To · learn · more · about · a · subject, · you · can · look · up · these · sources · and · read · them · yourself.⸿

Tip · #31 ⸿ ➤

In · the · United · States, · the · copyright · has · expired · on · most · books · written · before · 1923. · This · means · that · these · books · are · free · to · the · public. · The · site · archive.org · has · digital · copies · of · many · old · books.⸿

Libraries are a good place to start finding books, but they are not the only place. Books are increasingly available online as e-books. As with any other source, it's always a good idea to ask for help if you're having trouble finding a book you need.

Tip · #32 ¶ ➤

Local · libraries · are · great, · but · sometimes · they · might · not · have · a · book · you · need. · Don't · despair—some · libraries · might · be · able · to · order · the · book · for · you · from · another · library. · Ask · your · librarian!¶

Internet Research

The Internet is an incredibly useful tool. It has increased massively the amount of information accessible to normal people on an everyday basis. However, while the Internet is full of information, it is also full of misinformation. As a researcher, you want to ensure that you don't repeat misinformation in your paper.

Tip · #33 ¶ ➤

Remember, · the · Internet · is · a · place · where · anyone · can · post · anything. · If · you · are · writing · a · research · paper, · you · need · to · be · extra · careful · about · using · material · you · find · on · the · Internet.¶

You can't believe everything you read on the Internet

Luckily, it's typically not that hard to determine whether the information you find on the Internet is accurate. To begin, trust your instincts. If the information is from a sketchy-looking blog or website with no author listed, it's probably not accurate. Sites like Wikipedia are similarly unreliable sources, since anyone can edit them.

Tip · #34

Wikipedia · is · not · a · reliable · source, · but · that · doesn't · mean · it · can't · be · a · useful · tool. · Wikipedia · pages · usually · have · in-line · citations · and · suggestions · for · further · reading · at · the · bottom · of · the · page. · These · are · usually · good · sources— look · them · up · yourself!

Sites like Facebook or Twitter might not seem sketchy—you might use them every day—but they don't make good sources for a research paper. It's too easy for people to create fake profiles or falsify posts, so it's really not a good idea to use social media content as a source.

Tip · #35

Though · it · may · be · tempting, · avoid · citing · social · media · posts. · Even · if · the · information · is · accurate, · it · looks · unprofessional.

So what can you believe?
There is potential for misinformation, but that doesn't mean the Internet isn't a good place to do research. There are plenty of ways to find accurate information.

Tip · #36

Use · Google · Scholar · (scholar.google.com) · to · search · for · academic · articles · on · your · subject · area.

You can learn about a website from the letters it ends in. Among American websites, there are four common website endings: .com, .gov, .edu, and .org.

Tip · #37

Webpages · ending · in · .edu · are · from · colleges · and · universities. · The · information · from · these · sources · is · likely · reliable.

Tip · #38

Webpages · ending · in · .gov · are · from · the · U.S. · government. · They · probably · contain · accurate · information.

> Start with a basic Internet search and look for sources that have (or have had) a print equivalent. Ignore sites with a lot of advertising. .gov, .org, and .edu sites are normally pretty reliable. Look for bibliographies as well. If your information is sourced, it is likely a reliable source, and you have the added bonus of finding the sources they used.
>
> —Jennifer Thomas, veteran English teacher

Some people will tell you that you shouldn't trust websites that end in .com. Officially, .com stands for commercial. However, these days, plenty of reliable websites end in .com, including many major news sites. Articles from .com sites can be very helpful, especially if you are researching a contemporary subject. Use your best judgment and if you have any doubts, ask your librarian or teacher for their advice.

Tip · #39 ¶ ⬉

If · the · source · you · are · reading · on · the · Internet · has · an · author · listed, · look · up · that · person · and · see · what · you · can · find. · If · they · are · an · expert · on · the · subject, · then · your · source · is · probably · reliable, · even · if · it · was · published · on · a · .com · site. ¶

Websites ending in .org come from nonprofit organizations. Many of these are reliable sources—some nonprofits provide educational information, similar to .edu sites. However, nonprofits can also sometimes have agendas, and therefore show bias. For example, many political organizations register as nonprofits

Internet research is still research. The tools discussed earlier in this chapter still apply when you are dealing with Internet sources. You should always evaluate your sources for bias and fact-check one source against another.

Internet research tips

When you are using the Internet, try to stay focused on your research. It's easy to open up another tab to check out some website you really like— and then suddenly half an hour has passed and you haven't read a single article. You can lessen this problem by printing useful articles once you find them.

Tip · #40 ¶ ➤

If · you · have · access · to · a · printer, · print · the · sources · that · you · find · on · the · Internet. · This · way, · you · can · make · notes · directly · on · the · source · itself. · Plus, · if · something · goes · wrong · with · the · Internet · or · the · site · you · used, · you · can · still · access · your · source. ¶

When you are researching on the Internet, use a computer, not your cell phone. It is easier to take notes on a computer and you are less likely to get distracted.

Concluding Your Research

At some point, you'll need to finish the research stage of your project and start writing. For some people, it can be difficult to move on — when you conduct a lot of research, you often realize that there is a vast world out there full of things that you don't know. It can be difficult to accept that you have enough material and move on.

Remember, the goal of your research is to find enough information to form and support your thesis. If you have enough information to fill out a brainstorming chart or create an outline, you are probably ready to start your paper.

Chapter 4

Avoiding Plagiarism

Y ou've probably heard of plagiarism—it is a form of cheating, which unfortunately happens when students try to cut corners on research papers or similar assignments. When students are caught for plagiarism, they sometimes try to claim that they didn't understand what plagiarism was, and they didn't know their actions were wrong.

This chapter will give a clear overview of what constitutes plagiarism. After reading it, you will understand what it is and why it's a problem. From now on, when you write research papers, you will be able to avoid plagiarism—thus staying out of trouble and giving people credit for work that is rightfully theirs.

> Cite a source every time you write something that didn't come from your own head.
>
> —Sarah Seitz, Founder of "The Enrichery,"
> a comprehensive education company

What is Plagiarism?

The Merriam-Webster Dictionary defines plagiarism as "the act of using another person's words or ideas without giving credit to that person." Essentially, plagiarism is made up of two crimes. First, people who plagiarize steal the work of another person. Second, they lie about it by failing to give credit.

So what makes plagiarism different from quoting or using information from other sources? After all, you have learned that you are supposed to rely on information from other sources for your research paper.

Your work becomes plagiarism if you fail to acknowledge the sources you used. For example, the paragraph at the beginning of this section quoted from the Merriam-Webster dictionary. This is not plagiarism. The sentence makes it clear that the paragraph uses a quote—it is in quotation marks and is directly attributed to Merriam-Webster. Additionally, the Merriam-Webster page is cited in the bibliography of this book.

If the section had opened "Plagiarism is the act of using another person's words or ideas without giving credit to that person," with no acknowledgment of where that definition came from, then it would have been plagiarism.

Plagiarism isn't limited to copying from online sources. The following sections will explore a few other common instances of plagiarism and how to avoid them.

Tip · #41 ¶

Most · schools · have · strict · policies · about · plagiarism. · You · can · probably · look · up · your · school's · rules · about · it · online · or · in · a · student · handbook. ¶

[You should cite] anytime you are borrowing someone else's ideas (not just their words!). Even if you summarize or put a quote in your own words, you must cite. If what you are reporting is common knowledge (i.e. something easily accessible in three encyclopedic sources), you do not need to cite.

—Jennifer Thomas, veteran English teacher

Obvious plagiarism

Some forms of plagiarism are obvious. It is plagiarism to submit work written by anyone else—you can't borrow an essay your older sibling or friend wrote in the past. Asking a friend to write any part of your paper for you is plagiarism too. Even if a particular part of your paper is really tough, you have to write it yourself.

Failing to properly cite information is also plagiarism. If a source helps with your paper in any capacity, you must include it in a works-cited or bibliography page. Specific facts, like quotes, paraphrases, summaries, and statistics, typically also require you to use inline citations, which will be discussed later in this chapter.

Paraphrasing and summarizing

Sometimes, you will encounter incredibly important information in a source, but it won't be phrased in a way that works for your paper. When this occurs, you can either paraphrase or summarize the information — either way, you still need to cite it. If you don't cite something that you paraphrase or summarize, you have plagiarized.

Tip · #42

Paraphrasing · should · be · rewriting · the · author's · ideas · in · your · own · words, · not · substituting · a · few · words · in · a · sentence. · You · should · still · cite · something · that · you · paraphrase.

Let's say you're researching the Gettysburg Address, and you decide to paraphrase the following passage.

Original passage: "It is popularly believed that the battle of Gettysburg was the greatest battle of the War of the Rebellion. This may be true; but in the opinion of many competent to judge, there was greater carnage at Antietam and Chancellorsville was harder fought. Unquestionably, however, the battle of Gettysburg was the most important battle of the war from the standpoint of the success of the Union cause. Moreover, it was the only battle of the Civil War fought on Northern soil."[1]

Bad paraphrase example: Many people believe that the battle of Gettysburg was the greatest battle of the Civil War. This might be true, but other people say that there was greater bloodshed at Antietam and Chancellorsville was a harder fought battle. However, the battle of Gettysburg was the most important battle of the war because of the success of the Union cause. Plus, it was the only battle of the Civil War fought in the North.

This paraphrase is hardly a paraphrase—it changes a few words here and there, but it doesn't rewrite the passage. Including a paraphrase like this in your research paper would still constitute plagiarism, because you are practically quoting someone without attributing it as a quote.

Good paraphrase example: Although other battles, like Antietam and Chancellorsville, may have been bloodier and harder-fought, the battle of Gettysburg was more important because it was fought in the North and resulted in a major victory for the Union.

This second paraphrase is much better. Just remember—you still have to cite this passage, because you are taking another author's idea. Someone else said that the battle of Gettysburg was the most important battle of the Civil War. When you incorporate this idea into your paper, you have to give them credit.

---

1. J. W. Fesler, "Lincoln's Gettysburg Address," *Indiana Magazine of History* 40.3 (1944), 209. Web.

Tip · #43 ¶

Summarizing · should · explain · the · author's · ideas, · but · in · a · shorter, · condensed · version. · As · with · paraphrasing, · the · summary · should · be · your · writing, · not · the · author's. · You · should · still · cite · something · that · you · summarize. ¶

While paraphrasing refers to rewriting an author's ideas in your own words, summarizing means briefly describing an author's main point. A summary of the passage from the previous example would look like the following:

> Good summary example: The battle of Gettysburg was a more important battle in the Civil War because it was fought in the North and resulted in a major victory for the Union.

Tip · #44 ¶

If · you're · not · sure · whether · you · should · cite · something, · cite · it. · It's · better · to · be · safe · than · sorry. · If · you · are · able · to, · ask · your · teacher or librarian · for · their · opinion. ¶

Consequences of plagiarism

Students who commit plagiarism face serious consequences. In high school, plagiarism may only result in failing an assignment or a class. In college, a student who plagiarizes may be suspended for a semester or a year. In the academic world after college, people who plagiarize have their careers forever tarnished.

You might wonder, "If I just mess up with a sentence or two, will I really be caught?" You might be. Teachers now have access to many computer programs that can quickly run through a paper and see if its content matches up with other papers, books, and Internet sources. But even if your teacher doesn't choose to use such software, you should avoid plagiarism simply because it's wrong. You shouldn't take ideas from another person without giving them credit.

Citing Your Sources

Avoiding plagiarism isn't that hard—it just requires citing your sources. When you are writing a research paper, you will typically cite your sources in two ways. You will write a bibliography or a works cited page, which will list all the sources that helped you write the paper. You will also include inline citations, also called in-text citations, in the form of footnotes, endnotes, or parenthetical citations, to specifically mark quotes and places where you paraphrased or summarized a source. Inline citations allow a reader to match something you cited with its full works-cited or bibliography entry at the end of the paper.

> Always cite your sources. It serves two purposes: documenting the work that you have done to find that information, and providing credit to the one who wrote the original work. When in doubt, cite your source and you will look like a pro every time. Purdue University maintains an online writing lab that is useful for crafting your citations and references.
>
> —David D. Timony, Ph.D.

Citation styles

Unfortunately, there isn't just one way to cite your sources in a research paper. The way you will need to cite your sources will depend on your subject area and your instructors' preferences.

Tip · #45 ¶

There · are · many · different · styles · of · citations. · The · most · common · are · MLA · (typically · used · when · writing · about · literature), · Turabian · (typically · used · when · writing · about · history), · and · APA · (typically · used · when · writing · about · science). · Make · sure · you · know · which · citation · style · your · instructor · wants · you · to · use. ¶

This book won't delve deeply into how to cite sources in each different style. Citations require you to list the essential information about each source—such as the author, the title, the publisher, and the date of publication. You can find examples of citations for any style online, and libraries typically have reference books that provide more thorough explanations of how to cite sources. You can also count on your teacher giving you thorough instructions of how to properly cite using the preferred style.

Tip · #46 ❡ ⬉

Several · websites · claim · to · provide · citation · generators, · which · allow · you · to · enter · information · and · create · the · citation · for · you. · However, · these · generators · are · prone · to · mistakes. You · are · better · off · looking · up · citation · guides · and · doing · the · citations · yourself, · though · these · generators · can · serve · as · a · good · base. ❡

Inline citations

Tip · #47 ❡ ⬉

The · most · common · types · of · inline · citations · are · footnotes, · endnotes, · and · parenthetical · citations. · · Check · with · your · teacher · to · see · what · kind · of · in-line · citations · you · should · use. ❡

Inline citations are also quite simple. The following are examples of parenthetical citations. Parenthetical citations go at the end of the sentence, and typically include the author and the page number, if available.

President Lincoln opened his famous address with the phrase, "Four score and seven years ago," a reference to the signing of the Declaration of Independence in 1776 (Lincoln).

Although other battles, like Antietam and Chancellorsville, may have been bloodier and harder-fought, the battle of Gettysburg was more important because it was fought in the North and resulted in a major victory for the Union (Fesler, 209).

Tip · #48 ¶ ⬉

Always · put · an · inline · citation · at · the · end · of · a · sentence, · regardless · of · the · piece · of · information · that · the · citation · refers · to.¶

Footnotes and endnotes are similar to parenthetical citations, but rather than including the author's name and page number in the line of text, you simply insert a number in superscript. With footnotes, you include the citation information at the bottom of the page, while with endnotes, you include it at the end of your paper. If you are introducing a source for the first time, you typically include the full citation information. If you've already used the source, you typically just list the author and page number. The following are examples of footnotes. A footnote is a citation style you will see throughout the book:

By the time Lincoln delivered the Gettysburg Address, his views on slavery had evolved from when he was first elected president. Lincoln now saw ending slavery as a moral issue.[2]

---

2. Richard A Katula, "The Gettysburg Address as the Centerpiece of American Racial Discourse, *The Journal of Blacks in Higher Education* no. 28 (2000): 110. Web.

Anti-slavery activist Frederick Douglas praised Lincoln, saying: "If an honest man is the noblest work of God, we need have no fear for the soul of Abraham Lincoln."[3]

Quoting and misquoting

Misquoting occurs if you incorrectly copy a quote from a source. Even if it's an accident, misquoting someone misrepresents their ideas.

Tip · #49 ¶

Be · extra · careful · to · avoid · typos · and · mistakes · when · quoting · from · a · source. ¶

---

3. Katula, 111.

Sometimes you might want to modify a quote to make it fit better within the text of your paper. You are allowed to modify quotes—you just have to indicate clearly to your reader what your modifications are.

> # Tip · #50 ¶ ▲
>
> If · you · want · to · modify · a · quote, · you · can · use · ellipses · (. . .) · to · cut · out · an · unimportant · phrase · or · brackets · ([·]) · to · insert · a · clarifying · word · or · make · something · grammatically · correct. ¶

Let's take the following passage from Lincoln's Gettysburg Address:

> But, in a larger sense, we cannot dedicate, we cannot consecrate, we cannot hallow this ground. The brave men, living and dead, who struggled here, have consecrated it, far above our poor power to add or detract. The world will little note, nor long remember what we say here, but it can never forget what they did here.[4]

You want to incorporate this quote into your paper, but it's a little long. You can cut it down using an ellipsis, as shown in the following example:

> "[I]n a larger sense, we cannot dedicate, we cannot consecrate, we cannot hallow this ground... The world will little note, nor long remember what we say here, but it can never forget what they did here."

Notice the use of brackets in the passage. When you remove the word "But" from the beginning of sentence, you lose the capitalization. You use

---

4. Abraham Lincoln, "The Gettysburg Address." 19 Nov. 1863. Web.

brackets to modify the word "in" to indicate that the capitalization is yours, not Lincoln's.

Check yourself

If you're worried about accidentally plagiarizing, the Internet can actually help you out. Sites such as Write Check (**http://en.writecheck.com**) allow you to enter your paper and highlight any passages that seem similar to other writing on the Internet and in many books.

At the beginning of this chapter, you learned about the variety of actions that constitute plagiarism. The consequences of plagiarism might seem scary, but avoiding plagiarism is really quite easy. Always cite all of your sources. If you're not sure how to cite something, ask a teacher or librarian.

Plagiarism doesn't happen by accident—as long as you are consciously trying to avoid plagiarism when writing your research paper, you will be fine.

Tip · #51 ¶ ⬧

Even · if · it's · late · at · night, · you · are · confused · about · citations, · and · your · paper · is · due · in · the · morning, · still · try · your · best · to · cite · your · sources. · It's · better · to · try · and · possibly · cite · something · incorrectly · than · to · skip · the · citations · and · end · up · plagiarizing. ¶

Chapter 5

Introductions

By now you're probably ready to begin writing your paper. You've done your research, constructed a thesis statement, and brainstormed ideas. It's time to open up a new document on the computer and begin typing.

Tip · #52 | ¶

You · don't · have · to · write · your · paper · in · order. ¶

You probably know the basic structure of a research paper. It begins with an introduction, continues with the body of your paper, and ends with a conclusion. The final version of your paper must follow this formula, but you don't necessarily have to write your paper in this order. Some people find introductions to be one of the hardest parts of writing a paper. If you find yourself struggling to come up with a clever first line, skip it and move on. You might find inspiration will strike while writing the body of your paper.

Tip · #53 | ¶ ➤

Avoid · distractions · while · you · are · working · on · your · paper. · Put · away · your · phone · and · stay · off · of · websites · that · might · suck · up · your · time. ¶

These days, most students write their papers on the computer. It makes sense—you don't have to worry about your handwriting and it's easy to make edits. However, it's also very easy to get distracted on the computer. Your mind wanders, so you go on the internet to check your favorite site for just a minute, but then you click on a video, and after it's done you click on another video . . . and an hour later you realize you haven't made any progress on your paper.

It's equally easy to get distracted by a cell phone or other electronic device. If you think your device might distract you, it's best to put it away completely—that way it can't interrupt your writing.

Tip · #54 ⁋ ⬉

Make · sure · to · save · your · paper · as · you · begin · writing · and · back · up · your · file · in · multiple · places. · If · something · goes · wrong · with · your · computer, · you · don't · want · to · lose · all · your · work. ⁋

Computers seem like really great technology, but they're not perfect. Sometimes they catch viruses or fill up on memory space or crash unexpectedly. If you don't save your paper, you can lose your work. Make sure to save your files so that they can be accessed from more than one place—if you were writing and your computer unexpectedly shut down and never came back on, you should still be able to access your work.

A lot of students like to store their files on the internet, using programs such as Google Drive, iCloud, or Dropbox. You can also back up your paper to a USB drive or send new versions of the file via email—there are a lot of ways to save your work, just make sure to use one of them.

Tip · #55 ⁋ ⬉

Writing · is · hard! · It's · OK · to · give · yourself · breaks. · If · you · find · your · mind · drifting, · stand · up, · walk · around, · or · get · a · drink · of · water. ⁋

If you haven't written a research paper before, you might be surprised to find that writing takes endurance. Don't try to write your whole paper in one sitting. Allow plenty of time and give yourself breaks, so you can refocus and do your best work. This also means you shouldn't leave your paper for the last minute. If you try to write it the night before, your options are pretty limited.

Tip · #56 ¶ ▶

Set · a · deadline · for · yourself · to · finish · your · paper · that · is · before · the · actual · due · date. · This · way, · you · will · have · time · to · revise · and · edit. ¶

You might think you're done once you've written the required number of pages. Actually, writing a first draft of your paper is a good start, but it's important to revise and edit your paper afterwards. Techniques for revising and editing your paper will be found in Chapter 8.

The next few chapters will address the various parts of your paper, and how to write each of them. This chapter is about introductions, Chapter 6 talks about the body of your paper, and Chapter 7 deals with conclusions. If you follow the advice in each of these chapters, you will come away with a complete draft of your paper. Good luck!

An Introduction's Purpose

Regardless of the subject of your research paper, your introduction serves a few basic purposes. First, your introduction should show your reader why your paper is interesting or relevant. You can do this several ways. You might connect your paper to a broader subject that everyone knows about. For example, if you're writing about the Gettysburg Address, you might remind your reader that the context for Lincoln's speech was the Civil War, an incredibly important part of American history. If your paper is examining a specific scientific concept, you might tell your reader about the implications of your topic in a field like medicine.

Your introduction must also set the tone and provide a roadmap for the rest of your paper. For example, if your paper is comparing two novels, your introduction should name both novels and tell your reader what about them you will be comparing. If your paper is analyzing the factors that led to a particular historical event, you should tell your reader the event and the factors you will discuss.

Tip · #57

Consider · your · audience · as · you · begin · writing · the · paper.

When you think about what you want to tell your reader, it's important to consider the audience of your paper. Often, your research paper may just be written for your teacher. Other times, you may be writing for your fellow students, or for a competition with unknown judges. The audience of your paper will affect how you write.

For example, let's say you are writing a research paper based on a novel you read in class. If your teacher assigned you the novel, you can assume that your teacher has read the novel too. If you are writing your research paper just for your teacher, you shouldn't have to summarize the whole novel—you can assume your teacher remembers the basic events. On the other hand, if you're writing about the novel for a magazine for students—who probably haven't read the novel—you might have to spend more time on plot summary.

The inverted pyramid

An inverted pyramid, or upside-down triangle, is a good rule to follow when writing your introduction. Just as an inverted pyramid is widest at the top and then narrows to a point, your introduction should start out broad and then narrow down to your specific topic and thesis statement.

Generally, starting out with broad statements to draw readers in can also help inform readers about background topics that relate to the specific issue you are writing about. A proper introduction needs to contain enough background material to allow the reader to understand the thesis statement and what will be argued in the paper.

Just as a paper can be divided into three parts—the introduction, body, and conclusion—the introduction can also be divided into three parts. The introduction should start with a hook, include a transition, and end in your thesis statement. The remainder of the chapter will discuss these three parts.

The hook

When you go fishing, it's common to place your bait on the hook. You throw your hook into the water, and the bait attracts a fish. Once the fish bites into the hook, it's stuck—which means you can reel it in. You've caught a fish!

Catching readers with your introduction is a bit like catching fish. The first sentence of your introduction is called your hook. It's supposed to lure in readers, so they bite and read the rest of your paper.

> # Tip · #58 ¶ ⬉
> Begin · your · paper · with · a · hook—a · sentence · that · is · intriguing · or · exciting, · and · makes · your · reader · want · to · learn · more. ¶

Example hooks

There's no one formula to writing a good hook. Some writers like to use shocking facts or statistics to open their paper. If your hook is surprising, your reader will want to keep reading to learn more. Below are a few examples of introductions that use shocking facts:

> According to statistics from the Bureau of Justice, over 100 million Americans have some sort of criminal record.[5] That is about one-third of the country's population. The large number of Americans with criminal records can largely be attributed to the War on Drugs, which began in the 1970s. The War on Drugs led the United States to lock up more criminals, leading to a massive growth in the prison population. However, many people who are in prison are not dangerous criminals, and keeping them locked up is expensive for taxpayers. Therefore, the United States should consider policies that reduce the number of people in prison.

> What works: Many people are surprised to learn that 100 million Americans have criminal records. This fact draws in your reader. This introduction then transitions well to the topic of the paper—why the United States should imprison less people.

> The Bubonic Plague—which swept through Europe and Asia in the fourteenth century—may have killed over one-third of the

---

5. "Americans with Criminal Records," *The Sentencing Project*. 2015. Web.

world population.[6] Better sanitary practices and the innovation of antibiotics have helped prevent another plague like that from happening again. However, the growth of antibiotic-resistant bacteria poses a serious public health threat and raises the specter that another disease as bad as the Bubonic Plague could strike again.

What works: A plague that killed one-third of people in the world is pretty shocking! Although this paper isn't about the Bubonic Plague—it's about antibiotic resistance —this introduction works especially well because the author uses the plague as a point of comparison, rather than just a "fun" fact.

Anecdotes, or short relevant stories, can also be good hooks. Some anecdotes are entertaining, while others can make a key point about your paper. Just make sure that if you use an anecdote, it is relevant to your topic. Some

---

6. M. J. Keeling and C. A. Gilligan, "Bubonic Plague: A Metapopulation Model of a Zoonosis." *Proceedings: Biological Sciences* 267, no. 1458 (2000): 2219.

students are tempted to use any funny or clever story, but if your anecdote is not relevant, it might confuse your reader.

Bad anecdotal introduction: When John Adams was at the Constitutional Convention, his wife Abigail sent him letters telling him not to forget about women's rights too. However, the movement for women's rights in the United States did not really gain steam until Susan B. Anthony became a leader in the 1800s. Although Anthony did not live long enough to see women gain the right to vote in 1920, her contributions to the women's suffrage movement were invaluable and she should be remembered as one of the most impactful women in American history.

What's wrong: The anecdote is this open attempts to tell the story of Abigail Adams telling her husband to "remember the ladies" in the Constitution—something he and the rest of its writers failed to do. However, this anecdote is confusing for a paper about Susan B. Anthony. Although Anthony's efforts ultimately led to more constitutional rights for women, this anecdote introduces too many people and makes the introduction confusing.

Good anecdotal introduction: On Christmas day in 1914, British and German soldiers decided to step out of their trenches not to fight, but to enjoy each other's company.[7] They had been fighting on opposite sides of the war for several months as part of the brutal World War I, but on Christmas day, they exchanged gifts, shared meals, played soccer and took photos together. The friendliness couldn't last—the next day, the soldiers were once again a part of opposing armies, fighting against each other in the names of their respective nations. World War I would be among the deadliest conflicts in human history, with over 17 million deaths. How did these

7. Robert M. Sapolsky, "The Spirit of the 1914 Christmas Truce," *The Wall Street Journal*, 19 Dec 2014, Web.

friendly soldiers become embroiled in such a conflict? The causes of World War I are complex, but can be understood by examining the two main factors: the growth of nationalism among European empires, and the strange alliances that these countries had created.

What works: The anecdote is detailed. It clearly relates to the writer's thesis about the causes of World War I.

Introduction clichés

You're not the first person to write a research paper introduction. Some hooks have been used so many times that they become overused and lose their effectiveness — these are known as introduction clichés.

Tip · #59 ¶ ➤

Avoid · clichés · in · your · introduction. ¶

Questions are a common introduction cliché. If you want to use a question to lead into your introduction, instead, try starting with a statement that leads into the question and then asking the question a few sentences into the introduction. Below are a few examples of question introductions, and how to revise them:

> Original hook: Would you know how to feed your family if you made less than $2 each day? According to the World Bank, 767 million people in the world make less than $1.90 per day.[8]

> What to do: In this case, the introduction includes a very compelling statistic. Skip the question and begin with the statistic.

---

8. World Bank. 2016. *Poverty and Shared Prosperity 2016: Taking on Inequality.* Washington, DC: World Bank. Web.

Revised hook: Nearly 11 percent of the world's population, 767 million people, make less than $1.90 per day, according to World Bank statistics.

Original hook: What if the technology your phone uses could also help reduce gun deaths? Several technology people have created something called a smart gun—a weapon that uses fingerprint technology to prevent accidental shootings.[9]

What to do: The question used in this introduction could easily be rewritten as a statement.

Revised hook: Technology developers believe that technology similar to what an iPhone uses could also help reduce gun deaths. They have created something called a smart gun—a weapon that uses fingerprint technology to prevent accidental shootings.

Quotations are another common introduction cliché. Some students try to begin their introductions with famous quotations that may have little to do with their research subjects. Here are a few examples of bad quote use in an introduction:

"Ask not what your country can do for you; ask what you can do for your country," said President John F. Kennedy in his inaugural address in 1960.[10] In fact, Kennedy's assertion in 1960 could easily be applied to Americans today too as the country struggles to address climate change.

What's wrong: The research paper is about climate change. Quoting President Kennedy might make the author sound smart, but it's actually irrelevant to the paper.

---

9. Nicholas Kristof, "Smart Guns Save Lives. So Where Are They?" *New York Times*, 17 Jan 2015, Web.
10. Ralph Keyes, "Ask Not Where This Quote Came From," *Washington Post*, 4 June 2006, Web.

"To be, or not to be, that is the question," wrote William Shakespeare in his famous play, *Hamlet*. Although this is the most well-known quote from *Hamlet*, Shakespeare's play is actually about much more than just this one line.

What's wrong: The research paper is about *Hamlet*, but quoting the "to be, or not to be . . ." line is a bit misleading and could confuse your reader. Furthermore, since everyone knows this line, it doesn't serve as a particularly good hook.

> Do not begin with a random quote ... this is CHEESY! Do not waste space in your introduction with plot summary. Teachers have already read your book. Spend time outlining your argument.
>
> —Sarah Seitz, Founder of "The Enrichery," a comprehensive education company

Occasionally, it makes sense to use quotations in your introduction, if the quotation is especially powerful and specific to your topic. The following is an example of an introduction that uses a quote but avoids being too cliché:

"Suddenly there was an enormous flash of light, the brightest light I have ever seen or I think anyone has ever seen . . . there was an enormous ball of fire which grew and grew and rolled as it grew; it went up into the air, and yellow flashed into scarlet and green. It looked menacing," scientist Isidor Rabi described the test of the first atomic bomb on July 16, 1945.[11] Although Rabi could see the

---

11. Edward T. Sullivan, *The Ultimate Weapon: The Race to Develop the Atomic Bomb*, (New York: Holiday House, 2007), 5.

pure physical power of the bomb, he had no idea about the geopolitical implications it would soon bring to the world.

What works: This quote is very vivid, so it will help draw in your reader. Since it's not well-known, your reader doesn't yet know what to expect, which makes it less cliché. The sentence after the quote helps pivot from the hook to the subject of the paper—the political consequences of the atomic bomb.

Metaphors or analogies are another way some students like to start their research papers. If your metaphor or analogy is original and specific to your topic, it can make a very effective introduction. However, metaphors and analogies can often become overused.

How do you tell if a metaphor has become a cliché? Ask yourself if the metaphor actually invokes an image or feeling in your head. If it does, then it's fine. But if you immediately know what the metaphor means—so that it doesn't give you any special image or new sense of meaning—it's probably a cliché.

For example, take the phrase "beating a dead horse," which refers to doing something useless or unhelpful again and again. This metaphor is used so frequently that it has become a cliché—when someone says this, people don't envision someone beating a dead horse. They just immediately assume the meaning.

If you are unsure whether your metaphor is cliché, ask around to see if other people have heard something similar before. Alternately, type phrases into a search engine and see what comes back. If a lot of people have used the same metaphor on the Internet, it's probably a cliché.

Completing your introduction

A hook isn't the only important part of an introduction. As you've probably noticed in the examples, the sentences that come after the hook help draw a connection between your hook and the point of your paper.

Tip · #60 ¶ ▲

Your · introduction · should · end · with · your · thesis · statement. ¶

You probably remember thesis statements from Chapter 2. The thesis statement tells the main point of your paper—you should have written it before you started writing the rest of your paper. You also have to place your thesis statement in your paper. If you are following the inverted pyramid method, your thesis statement is the narrow part. Therefore, it makes sense to put your thesis statement at the end of your introduction.

Using your introduction to provide context

What goes between your hook and your thesis statement? Depending on the topic of your paper, you might just use a few quick transition sentences. You might also use the introduction to provide context about your topic.

For example, Colombian author Gabriel García Márquez wrote the novel *Chronicle of a Death Foretold* based on real events that happened in the Colombian town of Sucre.[12] If you are writing a research paper about Márquez and this novel, you might want to provide some of this historical context. The next example shows a good way to do this.

---

12. Tom Phillips, "Nobel author Gabriel García Márquez wins 17-year legal fight over murder classic," *The Guardian*, 30 Nov 2011, Web.

Colombian author and journalist Gabriel García Márquez is known for his works of fiction, but the novel *Chronicle of a Death Foretold* isn't so fictional. Márquez based his story on the 1951 murder of a medical student named Cayetano Gentile Chimento in the town of Sucre, who was killed in a manner similar to the novel's protagonist, Santiago Nasar. The factual basis of the novel works alongside Márquez's use of magical realism to illustrate the varying ways people manipulate their interpretation of reality in response to tragedy.

No matter the topic of your paper, you'll always want to provide some sort of context in your introduction. The next example showcases another full introduction, this time about the Gettysburg Address.

American history is full of conflict—the country was founded by a bunch of rebels who were fed up with England, and the system of democracy that has persisted since our nation's founding is based on the idea that competing ideas will ultimately lead to the best solution. But the very core of this democracy was tested by the Civil War when a fight over slavery literally tore the nation apart. The Battle of Gettysburg, which took place in the midst of the war, was one of its deadliest battles and showcased the horrors of America's deep conflict. A few months later, President Abraham Lincoln was tasked with speaking at the dedication of a memorial in Gettysburg, and his two-and-a-half minute speech would later become one of the most famous in history. President Lincoln delivered the Gettysburg Address following the horrific Battle of Gettysburg to redefine the Civil War as not only a conflict between sides, but a struggle for justice. Lincoln's commitment to human equality came after his own personal reflections on slavery, and can be seen in his speech through his allusions to America's founding principles, as outlined in the Declaration of Independence.

Remember the basics

As noted at the beginning of the chapter, your introduction doesn't have to be the part of your paper you write first. However, it will almost certainly be the first part of your paper that your reader looks at. First impressions matter—you want your introduction to be good.

If unsure about how to tackle your introduction, remember the three basic parts: hook, transition, and thesis statement. If you're unsure of how to come up with a hook, think about something in your research that you found interesting or funny or strange. Chances are, your readers will feel the same way.

Chapter 6

The Body

Even for a long research paper, your introduction and conclusion will likely only take up a few paragraphs each, at most. The rest of your paper is the body, where you convey evidence to support your thesis. The evidence you use in the body of your paper should come from the research you have already done. It's a good idea to keep your research notes and your brainstorming close when you are writing—that way, you don't forget important information.

Tip · #61 ❡ ➤

If · you · find · you · are · confused · or · are · writing · the · same · thing · over · and · over · again, · go · back · and · look · at · your · research · and · your · brainstorming. · Don't · waste · your · time · writing · when · you · don't · know · what · you · want · to · say. ❡

Supporting Your Thesis

The entire purpose of the body of your paper is to support your thesis statement. Your thesis statement was just a statement — You told your reader what to believe. The rest of your paper is about showing your reader why you were right. Depending on your topic, there are many ways you can do this—using quotes, logic, storytelling, statistics, or all of these and more.

Backing up your claims

When you've done your research well, you should have no trouble backing up your thesis. After all, you wrote your thesis based on your informed research. Still, even if you have a very good intuition for why your thesis is correct, some students struggle to explain their arguments in a research paper.

The way to make sure you are backing up your claims is by constantly asking yourself the important question: "Why is this true?"

For each point in your paper, ask yourself why that point is true. Then, write the specific details that support your point in relation to your thesis. Your research should provide these details—look at your notes! Each opinion you plan on presenting in your paper should have one, if not several, specific details to support it. Details matter because you must show readers why your point is valid rather than simply telling them they should believe what you are saying.

For example, say you're writing a paper about climate change. Your thesis is that governments should limit carbon emissions to help slow the rate of climate change. Your first claim is that humans have caused the planet to get warmer. Why is this true? You can cite scientific data about the warming of the planet. You can explain scientific processes, such as the greenhouse effect, that seem to be causing this warming. You could quote well-renowned scientists saying that climate change is a real problem. These quotes, data, and logic are your evidence —they work together to support your claim that climate change is human-caused, which helps support your thesis.

When you are incorporating details from your notes into your paper, don't forget to include citations! If you are unsure how to cite something, indicate to yourself somehow (for example, buy using a brightly-colored font) that you must still insert a citation. This way, you don't forget to cite something and accidentally plagiarize. If you need a refresher on citations or plagiarism, refer to Chapter 4.

Structuring Your Paper

Organization is essential to any good research paper. You must present your ideas in a way that your reader can easily follow and understand. This next section will address the various strategies you can use to structure your paper, and the situations where each one might work best.

Often, the best way to determine the structure of your paper is to first write an outline. An outline can help you determine the order of your ideas and their relation to one another. For more on how to make an outline, refer back to Chapter 2. If you've already written an outline, you are on your way to a well-organized paper!

> Draft your thesis and topic sentences from an outline. Be sure they are arranged in an order that makes sense. This becomes the backbone of your essay. Look to see how your sources organize the material. Use the source's table of contents, headings, and subheadings to figure this out. Be sure keywords from your thesis appear in your topic sentences so your ideas are clear and unified.
>
> —Jennifer Thomas, veteran English teacher

How should you organize your ideas?

Sometimes your teacher might have a very specific idea for how they'd like you to structure your paper. Many scientific papers, for example, follow a standard structure. Make sure to read your assignment and rubric carefully to see if your teacher requires a certain structure.

The purpose of structure is to make sure your reader doesn't get confused. You can test your paper for structure by reading it through and asking yourself whether there are places where a reader wouldn't have enough information. If the answer is yes, you probably need to add more information or change the order of ideas in your paper.

Chronological

If your paper involves telling a story or explaining events, it probably is a good idea to make it chronological—telling things in the order that they happened. Most history papers should be structured chronologically, as they typically involve events that happened in some succession. A chronologically-organized paper is also a good way to showcase cause and effect. If you are trying to prove that one thing caused another, it's important to give your reader a clear idea of the timing.

If you are planning on writing your paper chronologically, you might try writing a timeline or bullet points with key events as part of your brainstorming. You can use this timeline as a template when you begin writing your actual paper.

Comparing different ideas

Some research papers may ask you to compare different ideas and come to a conclusion. The structure of your paper can reflect these comparisons. For example, if you are asked to analyze two different novels for a paper, you might divide the body of your paper into three sections, analyzing the first novel, the second novel, and the similarities or differences between them.

Structuring your paper around comparison also works well if you are asked to analyze cause-and-effect. For example, if you were writing a paper about the factors that led to the 2008 recession, you could pick three factors based on your research that led to the recession. In your paper, you would analyze each of these factors individually, and then conclude the body of your paper with a discussion about which factors were most impactful and how each related to the other ones.

Tip · #62 ¶ ▚

If · your · paper · is · very · long, · you · can · break · it · down · into · sections · or · mini-chapters. ¶

Paragraphing

You've certainly written paragraphs before. An effective paragraph in a research paper should have four elements: a topic sentence, a coherent progression, supporting details, and an ending transition.

The topic sentence is the first sentence of your paragraph. It should give the reader a general idea of what the paragraph will discuss. The rest of the sentences in your paragraph should generally fall under the umbrella of your topic sentence.

A good paragraph should have at least three supporting details. Some paragraphs may have more than this, but three is a good number to aim for. If you cannot come up with three supporting details, then you will either need to do more research or adjust the topic of your paragraph.

It's important that your paragraph flows cleanly between these supporting details. Ask yourself what is the most logical order for presenting the ideas? Sometimes, certain ideas may rely on one another. If you are summarizing historical events or the plot of a book, it probably makes sense to present your ideas in chronological order.

Tip · #63 ¶

As · a · general · rule, · stick · to · one · idea · per · paragraph. · Obviously, · your · sentences · will · provide · more · details · on · your · topic, · but · if · you · find · yourself · talking · about · a · new · idea, · it's time to start a new paragraph.¶

Transitions, transitions, transitions!

Transitions are essential to any paper—they help guide the reader from one idea to the next. You typically use transitions between each paragraph in a paper. Some transitions (such as "additionally" or "likewise") indicate that you will be staying with the same idea. Others (such as "by contrast" or "on the other hand") indicate that you will be bringing up a different idea. Transitions can also describe a different time or place. Take a look at the list of transitions below, and see if you can think of any others to add!

Common transition words and phrases:

- Additionally

- Likewise

- In addition

- Similarly

- Furthermore

- Moreover

- As well as

- Therefore

- Unlike

- By contrast

- On the other hand

- However

- After

- Following

- Ultimately

- Finally

> # Tip · #64| ¶ ↖
>
> Use · transitions · to · guide · your · reader — don't · just · skip · from · one · idea · to · the · next. ¶

Include transitions between every paragraph in your paper so it flows together neatly. Try to vary your transitions, so that you don't become repetitive. Transition words aren't the only way to indicate you are moving from one idea to the next. For example, you can use a few key words from the last sentence of a paragraph in the topic sentence of the next paragraph to link them together. This creates a link between the information in the mind of the reader and shifts to a new point without feeling abrupt or causing confusion.

> "Instead of spending too much time on your transitions in the initial stages, allow yourself to write the rough draft and return later to muse over these sections. Generally, a successful transition combines an idea from the former that connects to the latter and shows a logical flow of ideas."
>
> —Jen Garcia, licensed mental health counselor

Transitions that use transition words are known as direct transitions. Transitions that guide the reader from one point to another without using key transition words are known as indirect transitions. The following example, from a paper about historical immigration between the United States and Mexico, showcases a direct transition:

. . . The proximity between the United States and Mexico made it easy for immigrant workers to come to the United States only temporarily. Mexican immigration records from 1911 and 1912 show that the number of Mexicans who immigrated to the United States in those years was roughly the same as the number who returned to Mexico.

However, the Mexican Revolution led to a decline in the reciprocity of immigration between the United States and Mexico. The conflict, especially following the assassination of President Francisco Madero in 1913, resulted in an influx of migrants and refugees from Mexico to the United States.

This example uses the transition word "however" to indicate that the pattern described in the previous paragraph will change. The same transition could also be written indirectly, as shown in the next example:

. . . The proximity between the United States and Mexico made it easy for immigrant workers to come to the United States only temporarily. Mexican immigration records from 1911 and 1912 show that the number of Mexicans who immigrated to the United States in those years was roughly the same as the number who returned to Mexico—a reciprocal pattern of immigration.

Reciprocity resulting from temporary immigration declined as a result of the Mexican Revolution. The conflict, especially following the assassination of President Francisco Madero in 1913, resulted in an influx of migrants and refugees from Mexico to the United States.

This example works well because the first sentence of the second paragraph uses two words "reciprocity" and "temporary" which clearly tie it to the previous paragraph. No transition word is necessary.

Writing Style

The structure of your paper helps make sure your ideas are easy to follow. The other essential component to making your work readable is writing style. The remainder of this chapter will consider how to write sentences that sound good, weave those sentences into paragraphs, and incorporate quotes and evidence.

Research paper style

The tone of your paper refers to your attitude toward your reader, which you show through your word choices. For example, the tone of this book is fairly informal. The book directly addresses you, the reader. It uses contractions and sometimes exclamation points.

Tip · #65 ¶ ⬉

Avoid · using · contractions · when · writing · a · research · paper. ¶

The tone of your research paper should generally be formal. This means you should avoid contractions, which are considered informal, because they mimic how people speak. You should also avoid exclamation points, as well as words like "I," "you," and "we." Research papers are focused on ideas — using the first or second person emphasizes yourself or your reader, whereas you want the focus to be on your arguments and evidence.

Tip · #66 ¶ ⬉

Try · to · avoid · using · the · first · person · ("I") · and · the · second · person · ("you") · when · writing · a · research · paper. ¶

NEVER EVER WRITE: "In this paper, I am going to tell you about . . ."

This is in first person — you should be writing in 3rd person! Plus, it sounds LAME! Stay in the present tense . . . pretend it is happening right now.

—Sarah Seitz, Founder of "The Enrichery,"
a comprehensive education company

Some teachers have very specific styles they want you to follow. Make sure to check your rubric or assignment guide, and ask your teacher about their preferences.

Word choice

Research papers ask you to write more formally than you have in the past. Some students make the mistake of trying to sound impressive and professional by using very long and fancy words. As a general rule, it's OK to use a thesaurus to brainstorm synonyms for a word you think you might be overusing, but you shouldn't write a word in your essay if you aren't 100 percent certain about what it means.

For example, don't write: "The numerical mean temperature evaluated at disparate locations across the globe has flourished upward at a reliable rate during the course of the last half-century," when you really mean: "The average global temperatures have increased steadily over the last 50 years."

Types of sentences

You probably think you know a lot about sentences. You've definitely written sentences before—which makes writing your paper much easier. After all, research papers are made up of many sentences. While anyone can write many sentences, not all sentences are created equally. This section will go over the various kinds of sentences, and how to use each of them effectively in your paper.

Simple sentences

Sentences are made up of clauses, which have one or more subject and verb. A simple sentence has just one clause. Take a look at a few examples of simple sentences:

Sally took her dog to the park.

President Abraham Lincoln delivered the Gettysburg Address following the Battle of Gettysburg.

Global temperatures have trended upwards over the last 50 years.

The British and German soldiers played soccer and took pictures together.

Note this last example, which is still only one clause. The British and German soldiers are together the subject. The clause has two verbs — "played" and "took" — however, since both of these verbs reference the same subject, they are still part of the same clause.

Compound sentences

A compound sentence is made up of two or more clauses, connected by a coordinating conjunction. The clauses in a compound sentence must be independent, meaning that they could each stand on their own. You can remember the seven coordinating conjunctions using the acronym FANBOYS: for, and, no, but, or, yet and so.

The following are a few examples of compound sentences:

The general knew the attack was unlikely to succeed, yet he still tried.

The wise student backed up his work in several places, for he knew his computer might crash at any moment.

The Federal Reserve was worried about the market for Mortgage-Backed Securities, so they decided to intervene and buy billions of dollars of securities.

The British soldiers played soccer and the German soldiers took pictures.

Note how this last example differs from the one in the previous section. This time, there are two clauses — "The British soldiers played soccer" and "the German soldiers took pictures." Each of these clause could be their own simple sentence. When connected by a coordinating conjunction, they form a compound sentence.

Tip · #67 ¶ ⬉

Don't · start · sentences · with · coordinating · conjunctions. ¶

When people talk, they often start sentences with coordinating conjunctions. Think of any time your parent has told you something you didn't like and you've responded with the word "but." Since a research paper is more formal than these everyday conversations, avoid using coordinating conjunctions at the beginning of sentences when you are writing.

Complex sentences

Complex sentences are made up of multiple clauses, like compound sentences. However, complex sentences are typically composed of one independent clause and one dependent clause. A dependent clause begins with a subordinating conjunction. It cannot stand on its own as a sentence. The following are a few examples of complex sentences, with the subordinating conjunction underlined:

Although the general knew about the dangers, he still decided to attack.

Before the flood wrecked all the fields, the farmers in the area had successfully grown corn for 40 years.

The English and German soldiers spent time together, <u>even though</u> they both knew they would have to fight against each other the next day.

The quantity of carbon emissions has substantially increased <u>since</u> the world began consuming fossil fuels.

Complex-compound sentences

Complex-compound sentences typically have three clauses, connected by both a coordinating and subordinating conjunction. Take a look at the following examples and identify the conjunctions in each:

Although the general knew about the dangers, he still decided to attack and many men were killed.

After the flood washed away the corn fields, some of the farmers tried to rebuild and others decided to leave for the city.

Even though the English and German soldiers enjoyed spending time together, their countries continued to be at war and they had to fight each other the very next day.

Because humans have used many fossil fuels, the carbon dioxide in the atmosphere has increased and the planet is getting warmer.

Tip · #68 ¶ ▸

Use · a · mix · of · simple, · complex, · compound, · and · complex-compound · sentences. ¶

Why is it important to know about different types of sentences? Research papers are very long. If you always use the same kind of sentence, your work will get very repetitive. If you use too many simple sentences, your writing will seem short and harsh. If you only use complex-compound sentences, your writing will seem wordy.

As you might have noticed in some of the examples, the same idea can often be expressed in different ways using different sentence structures. Be conscious of the different sentence structures you can use, and your writing will improve.

Rhetorical questions

A rhetorical question is a question that someone asks without expecting an answer. Any question you ask in your paper will be rhetorical, because you aren't actually there to have a conversation with your reader.

Tip · #69 ¶

Don't · use · rhetorical · questions · in · the · body · of · your · research · paper. ¶

Rhetorical questions can occasionally be effective in introductions or conclusions, but they don't work as well in the body of your paper. You should be presenting evidence to back up your thesis—not asking your reader questions. The following example showcases a passage that uses a rhetorical question, and shows how to create the same effect without using a question:

> The colonial rebel army, though lacking resources, trained officers, and the backing of a formal government, somehow managed to

defeat the great British Empire. How did they do that? Several factors were key. First, the rebels were fighting on their own territory, whereas the British didn't know the geography very well.

Although the colonial rebel army lacked resources, trained officers, and the backing of a formal government, several factors helped them defeat the great British Empire. First, the rebels were fighting on their own territory, whereas the British didn't know the geography very well.

Passive voice

Passive voice and its counterpart, active voice, refer to who or what in a sentence is completing the action described by the verb. When a sentence is in active voice, the subject of the sentence completes the action described by the verb. When a sentence is in passive voice, the verb acts upon the subject of the sentence, and the person or thing who completes the action is described in a prepositional phrase, or left out entirely. If that sounds confusing, it's much easier to see active and passive voice through examples. Take a look below:

Passive voice: The ball was thrown by Bob.

Active voice: Bob threw the ball.

Passive voice: The trash was taken out at 7 a.m.

Active voice: Karen took the trash out at 7 a.m.

Passive voice: The battle would be remembered by all the townspeople as a long and grueling fight.

Active voice: All the townspeople would remember the battle as a long and grueling fight.

Passive voice: Tom Kirkman was named the Secretary of Housing and Urban Development.

Active voice: The President named Tom Kirkman the Secretary of Housing and Urban Development.

Tip · #70 ¶ ➤
Try · to · avoid · passive · voice · in · your · writing. ¶

Many times, the passive voice sounds awkward and makes your sentences wordier. More importantly, the passive voice de-emphasizes the person who completes the action, which can be confusing. In fact, writers sometimes intentionally use passive voice when they are trying not to reveal information—but you shouldn't do this in your research paper!

> "Let's clarify: the passive voice is not a grammatical error, and it is not something spell check will pick up. Passive voice happens within the structure of a sentence. It is about *how* you say what you are saying. Research papers, by and large, are intended to be clear, consistent, and factual. The best way to convince your reader (and your professor) that you have done the work and know what you are talking about is to avoid using passive voice. There are plenty of resources on how to recognize passive voice and change it. A simple online search will bring you helpful hints!"
>
> —Jen Garcia, licensed mental health counselor

The following are more examples of passive voice as they might come up your writing, and how you can fix them:

Passive voice: At exactly 1:05 p.m., the missile was launched.

Active voice: At exactly 1:05 p.m., the military commander pressed the button launching the missile.

Passive voice: The general thought he would be able to launch a surprise attack, but his plans were leaked to the enemy.

Active voice: The general thought he would be able to launch a surprise attack, but someone had leaked his plans to the enemy.

Incorporating quotes

Quotes are one form of evidence that most research papers rely on. Chapter 4 discussed how to properly cite quotes; this section will address how to incorporate them into the body of your paper. There are several different ways you can integrate a quote into your writing—which one you should use depends on the length of the quote and the context.

Tip · #71 ¶ ↖

If · you · are · only · quoting · a · few · words · or · a · phrase, · you · can · incorporate · the · quote · into · your · own · sentences. ¶

If you only want to quote a few words from another author, it's fairly easy to incorporate their work into your writing. Look at the following examples:

> In his Gettysburg Address, Lincoln shows respect for the founding father's ideals, describing America as a nation "conceived in liberty."[13]

> Mulisch uses auditory imagery to describe the horrors of the prison, as Anton hears "sudden cursing" and "the dull thud of a beating" while he sits in his cell.[14]

Tip · #72 ¶ ↖

If · your · quote · is · at · least · a · full · clause · (with · a · subject · and · a · verb), · it · should · stand · alone · grammatically · in · your · writing. ¶

Often, you will want to quote more than just a few words. If you are quoting a full clause or sentence, the quote should be able to stand alone in your writing. In these cases, you introduce your quote with a colon, as in the following examples:

---

13. Lincoln.
14. Harry Mulisch, *The Assault,* translated by Claire Nichols White, (New York: Pantheon Books, 1985), 37.

The Battle of Gettysburg was the most important of the Civil War, according to historian J. W. Fesler: "[The] battle of Gettysburg was the most important battle of the war from the standpoint of the success of the Union cause. Moreover, it was the only battle of the Civil War fought on Northern soil."[15]

Anton feels guilty when he returns to his family's old home after the war: "The criminal returns to the scene of the crime."[16]

Tip · #73 ¶ ▲

If · you · are · using · a · quote · that · is · four · lines · or · longer, · you · must · format · it · as · a · block · quote. ¶

Quotes that are very long are known as block quotes, and must be formatted differently. Like a regular quote, a block quote should be able to stand on its own grammatically, and should be introduced with a colon. Look at the following example:

In the final paragraph of his Gettysburg Address, Lincoln describes how the survivors must work to build a better nation:

It is rather for us the living, we here be dedicated to the great task remaining before us—that from these honored dead we take increased devotion to that cause for which they here gave the last full measure of devotion—that we here highly resolve that these dead shall not have died in vain, that this nation shall have a new birth of freedom,

15. Fesler, 209.
16. Mulisch, 62.

and that government of the people, by the people, for the people shall not perish from the earth.

Generally, you must use a block quote if you are quoting a passage that is four lines or longer. You should use block quotes sparingly—the purpose of your research paper is to develop your ideas and support them with evidence. If you spend too much of your paper on long quotes, you won't have much space for your own ideas.

> **Tip · #74** ¶ ↖
>
> When · you · include · a · quote, · you · probably · will · need · to · explain · it. · Don't · let · your · explanation · of · your · quote · begin · with · "This · quote · shows . . ." · or · a · similar · phrase. ¶

Quotes are pieces of evidence that support your thesis, but just stating quotes isn't enough. You also need to explain to your reader how the quote is relevant and supports your thesis. Each quote that you use in your research paper should be followed by an explanation that is at least as long as the quote.

As part of formal research paper style, avoid using phrases like "this quote shows." Just state the quote, and state your explanation, as shown in the next example:

> Anton feels guilty when he returns to his family's old home after the war: "The criminal returns to the scene of the crime."[17] Anton's belief that he is a criminal reflects his survivor's guilt that he feels as the only member of his family to survive the war. He was not the

---

17. Mulisch, 62.

one to burn down his family's home, but he nonetheless takes responsibility. Anton's personal struggle reflects the novel's theme of how society responds to trauma.

> # Tip · #75 ⁋ 🕽
>
> Remember, · a · quote · means · you · are · taking · the · words · and · ideas · of · someone · else. · If · you · are · using · a · quote · in · your · research · paper, · you · should · always · have · · a · citation · to · go · along · with · it. ⁋

(Maybe) not just words

Depending on the subject of your paper, you might consider incorporating visuals into your paper. For example, if you are writing about science, graphs or tables showcasing scientific results might be useful. If your paper is about history, you might want to include pictures. Check with your teacher—they may have very specific ideas on how or if you should include these visual aids.

> # Tip · #76 ⁋ 🕽
>
> Depending · on · your · topic · and · subject · area, · you · may · choose · to · include · pictures, · charts, · graphs, · or · other · visuals · in · your · paper. · Unless · your · instructor · tells · you · otherwise, · these · visuals · should · be · labeled · with · a · caption · and · should · be · referenced · directly · in · your · text. ⁋

If you want to include visuals with your research paper, you must make sure they are genuinely relevant. Don't just include a picture or a graph because you think it's cool—it must directly support your thesis. To ensure your visuals are relevant for your reader, you should directly reference them in the text. The next two examples show how you can do this:

Average global temperatures have increased steadily in the last 50 years. (See Graph 1).

The "big-eyes" style that Keane used in her paintings was unlike anything American art had seen before. (See Photograph 1).

Graph 1 would be a plot of average global temperatures over the last 50 years; Photograph 1 would be a picture of one of Margaret Keane's paintings. In both these cases, the visuals would help the reader better understand the writer's point.

> # Tip · #77 ¶ ➤
>
> If · you · didn't · create · your · visuals · yourself, · don't · forget · to ·
> cite · them!¶

Keep in mind

It might seem like you have a lot to worry about in the body of your paper—quotes, visuals, citations, and transitions. Rather than thinking of these elements as requirements you have to meet, think of them as tools you have at your disposal. You have done a lot of research; the body of your paper is about finding the best way to communicate everything you have learned.

If you get confused, look at your notes or your thesis to get yourself back on track. Otherwise, take a deep breath and write down the things you know. You're going to be fine!

> # Tip · #78 ¶ ➤
>
> Recognize · the · importance · of · your · own · writing · style. ·
> Don't · pretend · to · be · a · stuffy · academic · or · write · like · you ·
> think · someone · else · would · write. · It's · your · paper. · Let ·
> your · voice · shine · through. ¶

Chapter 7

The Conclusion

If you've arrived at the conclusion, you're probably close to being done with your paper. Congratulations! Although you might be excited to finish, don't rush your conclusion. The conclusion determines what a reader will remember from a paper—it's your job to make sure your reader takes away the right message.

Ideas in Your Conclusion

Chapter 5 introduced the inverted pyramid structure for introductions. One of the easiest ways to write a great conclusion is to reverse this formula. Conclusions follow a pyramid shape—they start with the main point of your paper and expand to something a bit broader. A general formula for a conclusion follows three basic steps:

1. Restate the thesis.

2. Reiterate the key points of the paper.

3. Explain why the paper is relevant in a broad sense or what the reader should take away from the paper.

Restating your thesis

Tip · #79 | ¶ ➤

Your · conclusion · should · restate · your · thesis · in · different · words. ¶

Your restated thesis should address all the same points as the thesis but also seem final, rather than introductory. This time, you are not telling the reader what you are going to attempt to prove; you are telling them what you have proven through the research presented in the paper.

Many students struggle to restate their thesis using different words. After all, students carefully pick the wording of their thesis statement the first time. The next few examples take two of the thesis statements from Chapter 2 and show how a writer might restate them in a conclusion:

Original thesis statement: Although some people claim otherwise, the global increase in temperatures since the 1950s has occurred largely due to human activities, especially the burning of fossil fuels.

Restated thesis statement: When examining all the scientific evidence, it becomes clear that the burning of fossil fuels has contributed substantially to carbon emissions, which have led to the global increase in temperatures over the last 60 years.

Why this works: This restatement provides the same information as the original thesis. The phrase "when examining all the scientific evidence" reminds the reader of the scientific evidence that the writer presumably presented in the paper, which makes the restatement effective for a conclusion.

Original thesis statement: President Lincoln delivered the Gettysburg Address following the horrific Battle of Gettysburg in order to redefine the Civil War as not only a conflict between sides, but a struggle for justice. Lincoln's commitment to human equality can be seen through his allusions to America's founding principles, as outlined in the Declaration of Independence.

Restated thesis statement: The Battle of Gettysburg was a brutal episode in the American Civil War. When President Lincoln spoke afterwards in his Gettysburg Address, his speech was not about the conflict between North and South, but on the continuing battle for justice and the fight to extend America's founding principles to all people.

Why this works: This revised thesis conveys all the same information as the original version. Its final clause—about fighting for justice and extending America's founding principles to all people—is fairly broad, which helps with the pyramid structure of the conclusion.

Going over key points

Research papers are usually very long! Just as the introduction provided a roadmap of what the paper would discuss, the conclusion should remind your reader what they have just read. If you're not sure what the key points of your paper are, take a look at your topic sentences—they should describe the important concepts in your paper.

You should be able to summarize the key points of your paper in your conclusion without going into too much detail. You can repeat particularly striking quotations or statistics, but try not to use more than one or two. The conclusion represents your closing thoughts on the topic, so it should primarily consist of your own words.

While summary is important, you want to make sure your conclusion isn't just summarizing. Some students make the mistake of simply restating what they already said in their papers and then calling it quits. These conclusions are weak because they do not leave the reader with a sense of resolution. Summarization is necessary to remind the reader of what the main points are, but it does not tell readers what they should learn and take away from the paper. Try to keep summarization to no more than half of your conclusion.

Avoiding new ideas

Tip · #80 ¶ ⬉

Don't · introduce · major · new · ideas · in · your · conclusion. ¶

This tip might seem to counter what you've learned—after all, earlier in this chapter, you learned that you are supposed to broaden from your thesis. The trick is to do both: you should expand from your thesis, but without broaching a completely new subject. For example, if your research paper has been analyzing a novel, you might address in your conclusion how the lessons from the novel apply in the real world. You wouldn't bring up other novels from the same author and suggest your reader check them out.

Sometimes students bring up new ideas in their conclusions because they think of new ideas while they are writing their conclusion. If this happens to you, go back and add these new ideas to the body of your paper.

Making it Memorable

A good research paper will educate its reader about a topic. A great research paper will leave its reader thinking for days afterwards, inspired to learn more. While a conclusion won't make or break your paper, a strong conclusion will help make your paper memorable.

> # Tip · #81
> Your · conclusion · should · make · it · clear · to · your · reader · why · they · should · care · about · what · they · just · read.

Many research paper topics seem abstract or unrelated to everyday life. A conclusion should show your reader how to apply the lessons from your paper. Ask yourself what you would like your readers to do in reaction to your paper. Is there an action they should take or something they should examine or investigate further? Is there a bigger issue that your research draws attention to? For example, a paper on energy conservation might encourage readers to add eco-friendly practices to their lives. A research paper on a political proposal might ask readers to write to Congress and voice their opinion.

Some papers may not call for such direct action. If you can't think of something concrete you'd like your readers to do, you can indicate how the information in your paper might help your reader think about the world just a bit differently. For example, if you've been analyzing a novel, ask yourself how the lessons from the novel might apply to your readers' life. If you've written a historical paper, ask yourself whether there are parallels between the history and modern society.

Loose ends vs. big ideas

Loose ends refer to unresolved questions your reader might have about your paper. You want to avoid loose ends as much as possible—while it is OK for your reader to be thinking about the implications of your paper afterwards, your reader shouldn't be left hanging because you left out information.

For example, if you have written a paper exposing a major social problem, your reader might be left wondering what they can do to take action. That's an important idea. However, if you fail to mention the number of people affected by the social problem, or if you fail to explain how it was caused, those are loose ends. Go back and add information to your paper.

Conclusion techniques

"Write the conclusion last. Wait, what? Obviously? No, seriously, write your paper. Edit your paper. Then write your introduction. *Then* write your conclusion. Both your introduction and conclusion share the element of summarization. Where your introduction makes a proposal and promises to give evidence 'here, here, and here,' your conclusion connects back to your proposal and reviews the evidence you've given 'there, there, and there.' It may be helpful to think of your conclusion as bullet points. Each bullet point should summarize a paragraph of your paper. The last few sentences should connect to your introduction."

—Jen Garcia, licensed mental health counselor

Tip · #82 ❡ ➤

Create · a · connection · between · your · introduction · and · your · conclusion. · For · example, · if · you · used · a · clever · hook · in · your · introduction, · see · if · you · can · tie · the · same · words · or · concept · into · your · conclusion. ❡

Drawing a connection between your introduction and conclusion is one way to make your paper memorable for your reader. The following examples take a couple of the sample introduction hooks from Chapter 5 and show how the same ideas could be used in a conclusion:

Introduction hook: According to statistics from the Bureau of Justice, over 100 million Americans have some sort of criminal record.

Concluding sentence: Criminal justice reform is not easy, but given that over 100 million Americans have a criminal record, it is necessary.

Introduction hook: The Bubonic Plague—which swept through Europe and Asia in the fourteenth century—may have killed over one-third of the world population.

Concluding sentence: Governments should take the problem of antibiotic resistance seriously—after all, nobody wants another Bubonic Plague.

Tip · #83 ⸴ ➤

End · your · conclusion · with · a · memorable · line. ⸴

The final line of your conclusion is like the final bite of dessert your reader takes—they will remember the flavor for a long time after. You want to make this last bite as tasty as possible.

To make your last line strong, you should watch out for a few key characteristics. First, your last line should be definitive—don't use words like "maybe" or "perhaps" or "possibly," all of which indicate that you are uncertain. Your last line should also be broad. A broad last line fits with the pyramid strategy, and makes your reader connect your paper to the outside world.

Putting it all together

The following is a sample conclusion from a paper about the Gettysburg Address. To remind yourself what the paper was about, take a look at the outline for this paper, which was in Chapter 2. Although you haven't read the paper that would go along with this conclusion, see if you can identify which part of the conclusion restates the thesis, which parts summarize the key points of the paper, and which parts tell the reader what to message to take away:

> The Battle of Gettysburg was a brutal episode in the American Civil War, lasting three days and causing high casualties on both sides. When President Lincoln spoke afterwards in his Gettysburg Address, his speech was not about the conflict between North and South, but on the continuing battle for justice and the fight to extend America's founding principles to all people. Through his address, he redefined the Civil War as a moral battle over the issue of slavery, and called upon Americans to join the fight for equality. Although over 150 years have passed since President Lincoln spoke in Gettysburg, some people still argue that the United States has yet to achieve the "new birth of freedom" that the sixteenth president called for. Given the struggles our country still faces, perhaps all Americans should continue to follow President Lincoln's advice and "be dedicated to the great task remaining before us" — creating a better nation for all.

There you have it — if you've written your conclusion, you're finished with the first draft of your paper. Congratulate yourself, but don't print out it out and turn it in quite yet. The remaining chapters will discuss how to revise, edit, and format your paper, so that your final version is even better than your first.

> Conclusions are often the most difficult part of an essay to write, and many writers feel that they have nothing left to say after having written the paper (or they're so tired of writing, they rush the conclusion to get it over with). Keep in mind that the conclusion is often what a reader remembers best. Your conclusion should be the best part of your paper!
>
> —Sarah Seitz, Founder of "The Enrichery,"
> a coemprehensive education company

Chapter 8

Editing and Revising

Writing a research paper is a bit like racing through a giant maze. When you are in the maze, you can only make small decisions — do you go right or left? Sometimes, you run into dead ends and have to turn around. These mistakes are part of the process: if you stand in place, afraid to make errors, you will never get out of the maze, or finish your paper. When you finish the first draft of your paper, it's like you have made it through the maze for the first time. Even though you've completed your task, you probably didn't do it perfectly. Once you are on the outside, you can see the big picture. You notice your mistakes, and since this maze is really just a draft of a research paper, you have the chance to correct them. You might see that there's a much easier path than you noticed your first time through.

The process of making changes to the first draft of your paper is known as revising and editing. Some students neglect this part of the process: Many high schoolers don't finish a paper until the night before it is due or in a study hall before class, which leaves no time for revising. Other students will use spell-check as their only form of editing, even if they have time to be more thorough. If you are the kind of student who typically skips revising and editing, now is the time to break that habit.

Time is essential when it comes to revising and editing. Some students find it helpful to pretend their papers are due a day sooner than they really are, which creates extra time to revise and edit. If you have time, it's a good idea to take a break before you start editing your paper. If you are able to, get a good night's sleep, or even do homework for a different class. This will allow you to look at your paper with a fresh set of eyes, which will make you more likely to notice your errors.

I cannot think of a single classroom paper that I have written, or that I have read, that could not have been improved through revision. Revision is never a negative thing: even literary journals will request that their authors revise their academic essays. This does not mean that you should hang onto your paper and never release it to the world, but it is also important to acknowledge that we can all improve our writing if we look over our essays with an open mind.

—Laken Brooks, English teacher and curriculum developer

Tip · #84 ¶ ⭿

Ask · a · friend, · a · teacher, · or · a · family · member · to · read · your · paper. · Listen · to · their · suggestions · and · decide · what · changes · you · would · like · to · make. ¶

It can be difficult to be objective about your own paper for several reasons. First, your familiarity with your paper inhibits your ability to edit. Since you have read your own words so many times, you will miss errors because you subconsciously change what a sentence actually says to what it should say.

Furthermore, you probably wrote your paper in a way that makes sense to you. However, you are not the audience for your own paper. When you have written a research paper, you are likely close to an expert on the topic —you might not realize if you have failed to provide enough context or if your ideas seem out of order. Simply assuming that a reader will be able to follow your logic and argument can be risky, even when you have done excellent research. Editing and revising are about ensuring your paper makes sense to other people, too. Asking for other people's opinions is a good way to make sure that it does.

While it is a good idea to seek input from others, your paper still belongs to you. As the writer, you have final say in what changes you make. You don't have to follow advice from others, but you should be open to it. Some writers are so proud of their work—or so reluctant to make changes—that they refuse to listen to advice from others. Don't be stubborn or defensive. Take feedback.

Tip · #85 ❡ ➤

Always · look · at · the · rubric · or · assignment · guidelines · when · you · are · editing · and · revising. ❡

The editing and revising process is also a good time to look over your assignment rubric and make sure you didn't leave out any key parts. For example, make sure you have the proper number of sources, you have written the right number of pages, and you meet your teacher's other requirements. If you write a great paper but fail to meet some of the requirements on your assignment rubric, you won't score well. Forgetting aspects of the rubric is a silly way to lose points on your paper—don't make that mistake.

Editing vs. Revising

The words editing and revising are sometimes used interchangeably, but they have slightly different meanings. Revising refers to bigger changes in your paper, such as changing the structure or adding additional ideas. Editing refers to smaller changes, such as word choice, punctuation, and grammar. Because revising deals with bigger pictures issues, while editing involves little, specific problems, you should revise your paper first, and edit it after you are finished revising.

Chapter 2 of this book discussed thesis statements and the importance of the question, "Why?" When you are writing the first draft of your paper, you must argue why your evidence supports your thesis. When you are revising and editing your paper, you must ask this question again, but this time, you are not questioning your evidence or your thesis, you are questioning yourself. As a writer, why did you make the choices you made? Are there different ways you could've presented your information that might have been better? Answering these questions will help you think about the best ways to revise your paper, and help distinguish you from other students and researchers who might have written about the same topic.

Papers should be revised at least 2-3 times. Remember that revising means more than editing. When you edit a paper, you check for errors in grammar, mechanics, MLA, etc. When you revise a paper, you're checking for bigger picture things like sentence structure, flow, clarity of argument, etc.

—Sarah Seitz, Founder of "The Enrichery," a comprehensive education company

Questions to ask while you are revising

Revising your paper should address two main issues: the structure and content. Content refers to the ideas in your paper. Remember, the purpose of the paper is to support your thesis. Ask yourself, if the ideas in your paper link back to your thesis. Ideas that don't relate to your thesis can be distracting for the reader, obscuring the key points you want to make. While they may be interesting, your paper is probably stronger without them.

Do you have enough content?

To make sure you have properly supported your thesis, look back at your thesis statement in your introduction and break it down into its main points. Once you have a list of these main points, go through each paragraph of your paper and identify evidence that supports them. There should be several pieces of evidence for each main point in your paper.

If after reading your paper you realize that you have left some of your main points unsupported, you have two options. You must either rework your thesis statement to make it fit the points your paper actually supports, or you must add more evidence to the body of your paper to support your thesis. Either of these methods can work. Use your best judgment to decide which is more appropriate for your paper.

Content extends beyond just the facts that support your thesis statement. You must also make sure that your paper presents enough information and context to make your evidence understandable to your reader. Are there places where your reader might be confused? Is there additional information from your research you need to include? For example, a scientific table full of data might be important evidence in support of your thesis. However, if you don't explain what the data in the table means, your reader may be bewildered by all the numbers. Make sure you provide enough background information and explanation so your reader can understand the evidence in your paper.

Order and structure

Structure refers to the ordering of ideas in your paper. It is a good idea to look at your topic sentences—are they clear and specific? Do your body paragraphs contain evidence to support your topic sentences and your thesis? If your body paragraphs don't contain strong evidence, then you aren't adequately supporting your thesis.

You should also think about the order of your body paragraphs: Why did you choose that order? Now that you have written your paper, does that order make sense? Would a different order be better? Sensible order and flow to your arguments makes them far more powerful and persuasive.

Transitions are also a key part of structure in your paper, and something you should look for when you are revising. Make sure your paragraphs flow together smoothly, and that you aren't hopping too abruptly from one idea to the next. If you've forgotten how transitions work or need examples, look back at Chapter 6.

> A bugaboo for some students is misplaced information that may be important but has somehow glommed onto the wrong part of the paper. Proper placement of supporting information will improve flow and readability, which is crucial.
>
> —David D. Timony, Ph.D.

Editing techniques

If you have finished revising your paper and you are happy with its content and structure, you can begin editing. When you are editing, you aren't worried about your paper's thesis. Instead, you should be thinking about whether your words and sentences clearly convey your ideas.

Beyond spell-check

Many students think that editing is just about checking spelling and grammar. With computers and spell-check these days, editing almost seems unnecessary! But this is very untrue. Although spell-check is useful because it makes certain errors easy to spot, spell check does not catch everything. If you rely exclusively on spell-check for your editing, your paper will be left with some errors. For example, if you try to type the word "gear" but accidentally hit the "F" key, which is next to the "G" key on a standard keyboard, you will spell "fear." Depending on the context, spelling and grammar checks will likely ignore this mistake.

Mistypes and other mistakes like this happen often, so be sure to watch out for them while you are editing. When readers uncover grammar and editing errors, they tend to believe the research is lower quality and that the writer does not care about their work. You've worked really hard on your research paper—don't let people discredit you because of a spelling mistake or typo.

> # Tip · #86 ¶ ⸜
> Don't · trust · your · word · processing · program · to · edit · your · work · for · you. · · Editing · is · about · more · than · just · spelling · and · grammar. ¶

In addition to checking for spelling and grammar, editing means ensuring that your sentences are clear and your word choices are accurate. For example, Chapter 6 discussed how to avoid passive voice in your writing. When you are editing, you should look for sentences that are in passive voice, and switch them to active voice. Remember, active voice tends to flow better and makes your writing more vibrant.

How to catch your mistakes

Tip · #87| ¶ ▶

If · possible, · print · your · paper · and · edit · it · by · hand. ¶

You are probably used to looking at your paper on the computer—you've been doing that for many hours! Printing your paper will allow you to look at it with a fresh set of eyes. You can pick out a pretty-colored pen to make edits.

Making edits by hand also forces you to think more deeply about changes to your paper. You might notice something wrong with your paper when you are reading the print copy, and write down a way to correct it. When you go to fix your paper on your computer, you'll have to think about the correction again, which will help you come up with the best possible change.

Tip · #88| ¶ ▶

Read · your · paper · aloud · when · you · are · editing. ¶

Reading out loud requires a higher level of concentration compared to reading silently. You will remain more focused on the words that are actually on the page, which will allow you to spot errors more easily and will also highlight passages that are clunky or poorly worded. If you stumble reading a section, consider changing it so it rolls off the tongue more cleanly.

I suggest plugging your completed paper into Google Translate and having your computer read your paper to you. You can hear more mistakes, such as misspelled words or awkward sentence structures, when an automated voice is reciting your essay. Furthermore, avoid meandering sentences. Complex sentences have their place in any paper, but your argument will become convoluted when you have too many lengthy sentences. If you notice you have forgotten the start of a sentence by the time you finish reading it, you should shorten or otherwise simplify that sentence. In order to ensure that your paper flows from beginning to end, start reading your completed rough draft backwards, from conclusion to introduction. If your argument still makes sense and is persuasive, you have a strong essay.

—Laken Brooks, English teacher and curriculum developer

While following these techniques will help you edit your paper, editing is often easier if you know what sort of mistakes to look for. Many teachers will tell you that students commonly make the same errors in their writing. The next chapter will address these common mistakes, and give advice to help you catch them in your research paper.

Chapter 9

Common Writing Mistakes

As this book has mentioned many times, you are not the first student to write a research paper! This is good, because it means the mistakes that you will likely make when writing your paper are mistakes that many other students have made before. Even better, this chapter will outline these common writing mistakes and provide tips on how you can fix them creating an error-free final version of your paper.

Things to Watch Out For

One mistake many students make is overusing their favorite words. Maybe you like the transition word "however." Maybe you describe everything as "essential," or introduce every piece of evidence with the phrase "for example." Your reader will notice if you use the same words or phrases over again, and may become more focused on that word or phrase than your argument.

Tip · #89 ¶ ➤

Use · the · search · function · to · see · what · words · you · might · be · using · too · often, · and · then · look · up · some · synonyms. ¶

For example, let's say you overuse the word "often" in your writing. According to the thesaurus, some synonyms are: generally, usually, frequently, regularly, normally, typically, and repeatedly. Depending on the context, you can probably substitute these words—and therefore make your writing less repetitive.

Homophones

Tip · #90 ¶ ➤

Watch · out · for · homophones: · words · that · sound · the · same, · but · are · spelled · differently. · Spellcheck · won't · typically · catch · these · mistakes. ¶

The English language is full of homophones—words that have the same pronunciation but different spellings. You are probably familiar with many homophones, "see" and "sea," "plane" and "plain," and "read" and "red," for example. While these homophones are all fairly simple to understand, some homophones are more subtle and used less frequently. As a result, students are more likely to make mistakes. The following table contains examples of homophones that students commonly misunderstand. Keep in mind, this list is incomplete—if you are wondering about other homophones, look up a list online.

Commonly Mistaken Homophones	Correct Usage
Your and You're	"Your" is a possessive word indicating ownership. (Ex: Do not forget your movie tickets). "You're" is a contraction of the words "you" and "are." (Ex: Are you sure you're going to come with us to the movie?)
Its and It's	"Its" with no apostrophe is the possessive form of the pronoun "it." (Ex: The dog wagged its tail). "It's" is a contraction of the words "it" and "is." (Ex: It's a big dog)

There, Their, and They're	"There" is used to indicate a place. (Ex: Do not park there). "Their" is the possessive of the pronoun "they." (Ex: We got here in their car). "They're" is a contraction of the words "they" and "are." (Ex: They're bringing the car).
Accept and Except	"Accept" is a verb, which typically means to receive something. (Ex: I accept my mom's suggestion). "Except" is a preposition, indicates excluding something. (Ex: I accepted all of her suggestions, except the one about my thesis statement).
All right and Alright	"Alright" is a shortening of the phrase "All right." In your formal writing, you should always use "All right." (Ex: It is not all right to use "alright" in your writing).
All together and Altogether	"All together" means collectively, or at the same time. (Ex: We edited our papers all together during class). "Altogether" means entirely. (Ex: I am altogether too tired to keep editing my paper).

Who's and Whose	"Who's" is a contraction of "who is." (Ex: Who's the author of this great paper?) "Whose" is a possessive pronoun. (Ex: Whose thesis statement is this?)
Assure, Ensure, and Insure	"Assure" is to convince someone of something, usually in a positive way. (Ex: His mother assured him that everything would be all right). "Ensure" is to secure or make sure. (Ex: His mother ensured he had something to eat by bringing his lunch to school). "Insure" is to guarantee against loss. (Ex: His mother insured his car, because she figured he would probably crash it).
Which and Witch	"Which" is used as a pronoun, used to reference an unknown but specific subject, or used in parenthetic clauses. (Ex: Which cat belongs to the principal? It is the one which is on the table).

Which and Witch	"Witch" references a woman who stereotypically does magic, flies on broomsticks, and keeps a pet toad. (Ex: The witch invited us over for dinner, which we did not eat, because it contained maggots).
Weather and Whether	"Whether" is a conjunction, used to imply two alternatives. (Ex: Whether they win the game or not, we will be proud of how they played). "Weather" describes the conditions outside, based on factors like temperature and wind. (Ex: They will play the game outside, whether the weather is good or bad).
Then and Than	"Then" is typically used as an adverb to reference a time. (Ex: Back then, movie tickets only cost five cents). "Than" is a conjunction, used to compare two or more things. (Ex: Movie tickets are more expensive than they used to be).

Like other grammatical and spelling mistakes, misusing homophones hurts your credibility as a writer, and your teacher will almost certainly take off points for it. If you know a word is a homophone, or if you are unsure exactly which word to use, look it up! It's always better to spend a few extra minutes with the dictionary than have a silly mistake in your paper.

Grammar tips and tricks

Most students who are writing research papers think they have a solid understanding of grammar. You probably do—but there are some complexities of English grammar that students frequently misuse. This section will address some of these common mistakes and how to avoid them in your writing.

The importance of punctuation

Punctuation can be surprisingly difficult for high school students. Punctuation isn't just a matter of grammar—although you will certainly look foolish if you mess it up—but punctuation also affects the flow and rhythm of your paper. Knowing how to properly use various punctuation marks will make your writing seem smooth and professional, while misusing punctuation will likely annoy your teacher and cost you points.

Tip · #91 ¶ ↖

Be · very · careful · with · your · use · of · the · semi-colon. ¶

The semi-colon is a peculiar punctuation mark. Many students try to use them in place of commas or to connect items on a list. Semi-colons should be used in exactly two cases: when separating items in a list that already involve commas, and as a connection between two complete thoughts. Take a look at the following few examples, which show incorrect and correct semi-colon use:

Incorrect example: There were three finalists in the talent show: the girls who sang Johnny Horton's "The Battle of New Orleans"; the boy who rode his unicycle; and the group that danced to the song "1985."

Corrected example: There were three finalists in the talent show: the girls who sang Johnny Horton's "The Battle of New Orleans," the boy who rode his unicycle, and the group that danced to the song "1985."

Incorrect example: The committee narrowed down their search for new headquarters to the following cities: Poughkeepsie, New York, Denver, Colorado, Kalispell, Montana, and Los Angeles, California.

Correct example: The committee narrowed down their search for new headquarters to the following cities: Poughkeepsie, New York; Denver, Colorado; Kalispell, Montana; and Los Angeles, California.

In the first example about the talent show, the items in the list should be separated with commas, because the items do not already have commas themselves. The second example is also a list, but this time, semi-colons are necessary. Otherwise, it would be unclear for the reader whether "New York" referenced a city or a state. In this case, the semi-colon serves as a super-comma.

If you are using a semi-colon to connect two complete thoughts, you must be able to substitute a period in its place. Why would you use a semi-colon instead of a period? A semi-colon indicates a connection between ideas or thoughts in a way a period might not.

Incorrect example: John needs new glasses, he can barely read the newspaper in the mornings.

Correct example: John needs new glasses. He can barely read the newspaper in the mornings.

Correct example: John needs new glasses; he can barely read the newspaper in the mornings.

Now that you know how to use semi-colons properly, you might want to use them all the time! Resist the urge — semi-colons are best used sparingly. Because they connect sentences that could otherwise be separate, semi-colons speed up the pace of your writing. In certain cases, you may want to do this. However, if you use the semi-colon too frequently, your writing will seem too fast-paced, and your reader might feel rushed.

Tip · #92

Watch · out · for · fragments, · run-on · sentences, · and · comma · splices.

Run-on sentences, comma splices, and fragments are three errors that many students make, all of which have to do with improperly-written sentences. Run-on sentences occur when two independent clauses are connected incorrectly. Two independent clauses must always be connected with a period, a semi-colon, or a conjunction. (If you need a review on clauses or conjunctions, look back at Chapter 6).

If the two independent clauses are connected by a comma, the run-on sentence is known as a comma splice. Comma splices are fairly easy to spot because the clause before the comma and the clause after the comma will both work as stand-alone sentences. You can correct this error by adding a conjunction, changing the comma to a period and creating two separate sentences, or using a semi-colon. Take a look at the following examples:

Run-on sentence example: The general ordered the strike he thought it would help win the war.

Comma splice example: The general ordered the strike, he thought it would help win the war.

Correct example #1: The general ordered the strike; he thought it would help win the war.

Correct example #2: The general ordered the strike. He thought it would help win the war.

Correct example #3: The general ordered the strike because he thought it would help win the war.

Both the run-on sentence and the comma splice example are grammatically incorrect. The corrected examples show different ways the sentence could be written; each has a slightly different effect. Read through the correct examples again, and see if you can notice a difference in the pacing of the sentences.

> "Some of the most common mistakes in research papers are repeating the same phrase or word (especially a verb), using a conversational tone, writing in first person (I, me, my), writing in the second person (you, your), and unvaried sentence structure."
>
> —Jen Garcia, licensed mental health counselor

Fragments are the opposite of run-on sentences. A fragment is a phrase that is intended as a sentence but lacks a subject, a verb, and a complete thought. Some writers think that fragments can add emphasis, but in a formal research paper, you should avoid them. Because fragments occur when the writer leaves out the subject, verb, or complete thought, resolving a fragment will typically require adding something to your sentence. You can also resolve a fragment by incorporating it with the surrounding sentences. Take a look at the following examples:

Fragment example: The chains rattling as they fall.

Corrected example: The chains were rattling as they fell.

Fragment example: Running through the forest, leaping over fallen trees.

Corrected example: The boy ran through the forest, leaping over fallen trees.

Fragment example: The general was planning on ordering the strike eventually. Perhaps after the rainstorm.

Corrected example: The general was planning on ordering the strike, perhaps after the rain stopped.

Tip · #93 ¶ ⭡

Know · the · difference · between · a · dash · and · a · hyphen, · and · use · both · properly. ¶

Hyphens and dashes are two other fickle punctuation marks that you should make sure to study. A hyphen connects two words, while a dash separates phrases or clauses. Dashes are longer than hyphens, and dashes typically have a space on either side, while hyphens do not.

You always use hyphens when you are using compound adjectives — groups of two or more adjectives that come before a noun. Compound adjectives are hyphenated; however, a series of adjectives are not hyphenated when they come after a noun. Take a look at the following examples, which show when to use (and not to use) a hyphen:

My two-year-old cousin made me a birthday card.

My cousin turned two years-old last week.

I love this well-lit room!

The room was well lit.

Some words you know use hyphens all the time, such as "year-old" and "back-to-back." Any word that starts with "self" is always hyphenated, such as "self-care" or "self-esteem." You also always use hyphens before a number, such as "post-2000." If you are unsure about whether to hyphenate, look it up online or ask a teacher.

The rules for using dashes are a bit more flexible than the rules for hyphens. When used sparingly, dashes can add emphasis and make your writing more effective. Generally, dashes are used to accentuate a particular phrase or clause. You can use a set of dashes in the middle of a sentence, or a single dash to set off material at the beginning or end of a sentence. Take a look at the following examples:

Example without dashes: Many variables in both the United States and Latin America influence immigration.

Example with dashes: Many variables—in both the United States and Latin America—influence immigration.

Both of these examples are grammatically correct. The second example uses dashes to set off the prepositional phrase "in both the United States and Latin America." The dashes add more emphasis to this phrase and make it stand out. A writer would choose to use dashes in this case if this phrase was especially important.

Dashes can also replace other punctuation marks, such as periods. The dash typically makes the sentence or sentences stand out, as shown in the following examples:

Example without dashes: The general didn't order the strike. He thought the enemy wouldn't attack.

Example with dashes: The general didn't order the strike—he thought the enemy wouldn't attack.

Once again, both of these examples are grammatically correct. The example that uses dashes creates more emphasis than the sentence that only uses periods. Dashes can also be used to insert a clause into the middle of a sentence, as shown in the next example:

> *Example*: As the company has grown—it now has five times as many factories as it did in 1990—its environmental impact has also skyrocketed.

In this example, the clause "it now has five times as many factories as it did in 1990" provides additional information that is helpful to the sentence. Dashes are grammatically necessary in this case, because they set off the clause from the remainder of the sentence.

Dashes are a helpful punctuation mark, and can make your writing more effective. However, you should be careful not to overuse them. If you use dashes too often, then they will become less meaningful, and your writing may seem jumpy. As a rule, don't use more than one set of dashes in a paragraph.

Other writing notes

Tip · #94 ¶ ⬆

Avoid · using · an · unattached · "this." ¶

Improper use of the word "this" is another common writing mistake. When you are writing formally, you want to use the word "this" exclusively as an adjective, not a noun. When the word "this" is not followed by a noun, it can be difficult for your reader to tell what the word is referring to — a problem known as the unattached "this." Take a look at the following examples:

> *Incorrect example*: This is a very pretty table.
>
> *Correct example*: This table is very pretty.
>
> *Incorrect example*: This shows how the global temperatures have actually increased substantially since the 1950s.
>
> *Correct example*: This data show how the global temperatures have actually increased substantially since the 1950s.

Tip · #95 ¶ ⬆

Don't · confuse · "less" · and · "fewer." ¶

Writers commonly confuse the words "less" and "fewer." Both of these words generally reference a smaller quantity, but there is a key distinction.

Use "fewer" when the quantity you are describing is countable and the noun you are describing has a plural; use "less" when you would not be able to count the quantity, or if the noun you are describing does not have a plural. Take a look at the following examples:

There are fewer students in the class this year compared to last.

The fish tank had less water after George spilled some.

The Americans experienced fewer casualties during World War II than the Russians.

The new president spends less time in the White House than his predecessor.

The number of students in a class and the number of Russian and American casualties during World War II can be counted, so "fewer" is the appropriate adjective. The nouns "water" and "time" do not have plural versions, so you should use "less" in these cases.

The Power of Less

Philosopher and mathematician Blaise Pascal once wrote: "I would have written a shorter letter, but I did not have the time."[18] Although Pascal lived in France during the 1600s, his observation is relevant to many students' writing today. Good writing is usually short and concise. When you are editing and revising your paper, ask yourself: "Could I say the same thing in fewer words?"

---

18. Lombrozo.

The word count issue

Imagine you've almost finished your paper. You just need a few more lines—maybe your teacher wants a 12-page paper, and you're only at 11. It's really tempting to repeat yourself a few times. You could restate your thesis three different ways in your conclusion. Or you could add a few meaningless sentences to one of your paragraphs. Don't do these things. Every sentence—even every word—in your paper should be there for a reason, and that reason shouldn't be "I needed to add some stuff to meet the requirements." If you add material that is off-topic, it will distract your reader. If it is repetitive, your reader will get bored.

"Although it may sound counter-intuitive, write everything you've got down on paper *before* you worry about the word count. Until you know what you have, you do not know how to effectively edit it. Plus, you will spend more time stressing over the word count than the quality of your research."

—Jen Garcia, licensed mental health counselor

Tip · #96

Many · research · paper · assignments · have · word · counts. · Students · often · make · the · mistake · of · repeating · themselves · to · try · to · reach · a · word · count. · If · you · finish · writing · your · paper · and · realize · that · you · are · still · short · of · the · word · count, · go · back · and · add · more · examples · or · do · more · research · if · necessary. · Don't · repeat · your · same · points · in · different · words.

Writing concisely

So how do you make sure that every word in your paper means something? There's no one tip or trick that will make your writing smooth and concise, but there are a few guidelines you can follow.

Tip · #97 ❡

Use · strong · nouns · and · verbs · rather · than · lots · of · adverbs · and · adjectives.❡

You are probably familiar with adverbs—they are most words that end in –ly, and they are used to modify verbs, adjectives, or other adverbs. Adverbs are also typically unnecessary in your writing, especially in formal academic research papers. Consider the following example:

Wordy example: Global carbon emissions *increased very rapidly* following the Industrial Revolution.

This sentence has two adverbs. The word "rapidly" is an adverb modifying the verb, "increased." The word "very" is an adverb too. It modifies the adverb "rapidly." Both of the adverbs serve to strengthen the extent of the verb, "increase." In this case, the sentence could be made stronger and more concise by taking out these adverbs and using a strong verb, as shown in the next example:

Revised example: Global carbon emissions *skyrocketed* following the Industrial Revolution.

In this example, the strong verb "skyrocketed" eliminates the need for the adverbs. It makes the sentence more concise and powerful. If you are looking to reduce adverbs and use stronger verbs in your writing, you might find it helpful to consult a thesaurus.

> Using clear, concise language without overwriting is critical. Bigger words don't necessarily mean "smarter-sounding." Focus on your verbs and nouns. Concrete, specific nouns and strong verbs will strengthen your writing. This is a step that will come in the revision process, after you have all your ideas and structure nailed.
>
> —Jennifer Thomas, veteran English teacher

As the examples with adverbs show, using strong, clear words is better than using many words. The next few examples show other ways you can make your writing more concise by replacing a string of weak words with a few strong ones.

Wordy example: President Lincoln *talked about the importance of* creating a nation based on freedom and equality for all.

Revised example: President Lincoln *argued for* creating a nation based on freedom and equality for all.

Wordy example: The advent of the Internet *made available for the first time many things that people wanted to know about.*

Revised example: The advent of the Internet *gave individuals access to a new breadth of information.*

Wordy example: As a young man, Smith's work in the office of a famous New York lawyer *really helped make him believe that he wanted to change the world.*

Revised example: As a young man, Smith's work in the office of a famous New York lawyer *instilled his desire to change the world.*

You can also make your writing less wordy by relying more on nouns, and less on verb phrases. Take a look at the following examples:

Wordy example: The author's use of darkness imagery demonstrates *how the protagonist has become severely depressed because of the trauma he has experienced.*

Revised example: The author's use of darkness imagery demonstrates *the protagonist's depression resulting from his trauma.*

Wordy example: The experiment showed that *heated potassium nitrate released oxygen which reacts with the sugar and fats in gummy bears and blows them up.*

Revised example: The experiment showed that *oxygen released from heated potassium nitrate reacted with the sugar and fat in the gummy bears, blowing them up.*

These examples show just a few of the ways you can make your writing more concise. Ultimately, writing style varies from person to person, and there is no single rulebook for how to make your writing sound sleek and impressive. You should consider concise writing to be a goal—something you work to accomplish to the best of your ability.

"If you find you write too many words, look for repeated ideas/phrases and remove them. Then look for run-on sentences and shorten them. If you find you write too few words, ask yourself if there are there any concepts or ideas you have not explored and if there is enough transition between your paragraphs. Then ask yourself if you used all your sources. If not, is there a way to sprinkle in the unused ones?"

—Jen Garcia, licensed mental health counselor

Chapter 10

The Finishing Touches

If you like baking or eating, you might want to think about writing a research paper like making a birthday cake. First, you have to gather your ingredients—your evidence, your ideas, and your arguments. You mix them together, stick them in the oven, and come out with the first draft of your paper. The cake would taste pretty good when you pulled it out of the oven, but you can still do better. Revising and editing are like adding the frosting—minor modifications that make your final product even more appealing.

Now you've arrived at the final stage—the finishing touches. Maybe you use glittery icing to write "Happy Birthday" on your cake, or maybe you draw smiley faces or flowers. The equivalent stage in your research paper is finalizing your title and formatting. Those are the finishing touches. This chapter will address specifically how to complete these final stages of your paper, so you can make sure you turn in a great final product.

The Title

The title of your paper will be the first thing your reader sees, but in many cases, it may be the last part of your paper you write. While there's no specific rulebook when it comes to writing titles, the goal of your title is to engage the reader with your work. Some teachers like to see clever, funny titles. Others would rather that your title be straightforward and to-the-point.

Do not feel pressure to immediately come up with a title for your paper. I suggest waiting to title your paper until your paper is completed; that way, you have plenty of time to think of a witty or thoughtful title that will pull in your audience. When you come up with a title before you start writing your paper, you might feel reluctant to change up your paper if you find the topic deviating from your original title, even if this growth could make for a more interesting essay.

—Laken Brooks, English teacher and curriculum developer

A clever or funny title might engage your reader and draw them in, like a good hook in your introduction. However, some students try too hard to be funny and come up with a title that is irrelevant to their topic or argument. If humor doesn't come naturally to you, don't waste your time trying to make your title funny.

Your title should always be relevant to your topic and give your reader a basic understanding of what your paper is about. Your title should not be long—it shouldn't take more than a line on your computer. The following examples are hypothetical titles for some of the paper topics that have been discussed in this book:

"A New Birth of Freedom": The Purpose of Lincoln's Gettysburg Address

Fossil Fuels and Global Temperatures

From Rebels to Victors: How the Colonies Defeated the British Empire

Guilt and Trauma in Harry Mulisch's *The Assault*

As you'll notice with each of these titles, you should always capitalize the first word of your title. You should also capitalize all other important words—only prepositions (such as of, from, and in) and articles (a, an, and the) should be lowercase. If your paper is analyzing a particular document or source, you should give the name of the source and its author in your title.

Tip · #98

The·title·might·be·the·first·thing·your·reader·sees,·but·it's·not·actually·the·most·important·part·of·your·paper.·It's·nice·to·have·a·clever·title,·but·don't·waste·your·time·agonizing·over·it—the·rest·of·your·paper·is·more·important!

Formatting Your Paper

Most of this book has discussed the actual content of your paper—the words that explain your argument. The formatting of your paper refers to its appearance, which is based on factors like font, size, spacing, alignment, margins, headers, and footers. The citation styles discussed in Chapter 4 (MLA, Turabian, and APA) also come with formatting recommendations, which you can look up. Your teacher may also have specific formatting requirements. Make sure to look at your rubric or ask!

Why formatting matters

If you've already spent many hours writing and researching, taking the time to standardize your fonts and insert page numbers might seem annoying. By this point, you probably really want to be done with your paper. However, many teachers will grade your formatting. Even if they don't, a well-formatted paper is easier to read—and you don't want to make your teacher's life hard when they are reading your paper!

Tip · #99 ¶

Formatting · might · seem · silly, · but · it · does · affect · how · readable · your · paper · is. · Make · sure · you · use · a · professional · font, · such · as · Arial · or · Times · New · Roman. · Ensure · that · the · font · and · the · text · size · are · the · same · throughout · the · paper. · Most · teachers · will · tell · you · to · double · space · your · work · and · they · may · specify · margins. · Be · sure · to · follow · the · instructions · of · those · who · will · be · reading · and · evaluating · your · work!¶

Formatting your research paper is also a good skill to learn if you think you might want to publish your work someday. Think about if you've ever stumbled upon a website with annoying fonts or text that is too small. You probably didn't spend a lot of time reading it. Additionally, future editors or employers might ignore your work if the formatting looks unprofessional.

How to format

The software you use to write your paper (such as Microsoft Word or Google Docs) likely has all the tools you need to format your paper. Use the toolbar at the top of the document. If you're not sure about a specific formatting issue, you can always perform an Internet search: Typing in "How to insert page numbers in Microsoft Word," in your browser will yield some helpful results — you're not the first person to wonder.

Keep in mind that you might run into formatting issues if you transfer between file types (such as converting from Microsoft Word to Google Docs or vice versa). You should double-check your file extensions to make sure you are saving in a format that can be read by multiple programs, such as .doc.

Typically, your research paper should be double-spaced. You should use one-inch margins, unless your teacher specifies otherwise. Your font should be either Times New Roman or Arial. You should use size 12 font for your entire paper, although you may use a smaller size for footnotes or endnotes. You should indent every paragraph, but avoid extra line spaces between paragraphs. You should include page numbers, either in the header (the top margin) or the footer (the bottom margin) — your teacher might tell you which one. If you modify the header or footer of your document, those changes will appear in the header or footer on every page in the document, so make sure you are careful and intentional about the changes you make.

Tip · #100 ¶ ➤

Pictures · and · other · visuals · can · often · mess · with · the · formatting · of · your · paper. · Make · sure · to · look · over · your · paper · after · you · print · it · to · make · sure · everything · is · in · the · right · place · before · you · hand · it · in. ¶

The specific steps you follow to format your paper can vary between computers and file types. If you can't figure out a specific issue, ask a friend, a teacher, or a librarian. This also means you shouldn't completely leave formatting for the last minute—you don't want to be scrambling to figure out headers or page numbers the night before your paper is due.

When you are formatting your paper, you should also double-check your works cited or bibliography. Most citation styles require specific formats—and you really don't want to mess up citing your sources.

Afterwards

You print out the final version of your paper. Your ideas and research are in a final, tangible form. You staple your paper, place it in your backpack, and hopefully get a good night's sleep. The next day you hand in a final copy—you're done! You pat yourself on the back. You never have to think about your paper again!

Actually, you shouldn't give up all memories of your paper the second you are finished. You will have to write research papers again in the future. It's OK to give yourself a break once you've finished your paper, but it's important to take away some lessons too.

Don't stop learning

Turning in a paper that you are proud of is a very satisfying feeling. Finding out a few weeks later that you scored well is an even better feeling. But even if you've written a great paper and received a grade you are happy with, you still have room for improvement.

Tip · #101 ¶ ➤

When · you · are · finished · with · your · paper, · you · might · want · to · never · think · about · it · again. · However, · you · will · probably · have · to · write · similar · papers · in · the · future. · Make · sure · to · read · the · feedback · you · receive · from · your · teacher · or · instructor · so · you · can · figure · out · how · to · do · better · next · time. ¶

A good teacher will give you feedback on your research paper, even if you receive a good grade. Make sure to reread your paper and your teacher's comments. Take note, and think about what you can do better on your next paper.

In addition to the feedback you receive from your instructor, you should take some time to reflect on what you learned from the research paper process. You hopefully learned a lot about your research topic. You acquired skills, like using databases, writing thesis statements, and editing your own work, and you may also have learned something about yourself as a writer and researcher.

Writing research papers is about the process as much as the final product. Ask yourself, which parts of the paper were most difficult for you? If you struggled with research, you might consider whether you picked too narrow of a topic, or whether you should look for sources in other places in the future. If you had trouble writing an introduction, you should remember to allow extra time for it the next time you write a paper. Maybe you learned that you are most productive at a certain time of day. Maybe you discovered that you're not the best with deadlines. Maybe you got really good advice from a friend. Remembering these facts about yourself will help with your papers in the future.

Congratulations on finishing your research paper, and best of luck with future ones!

Conclusion

At the beginning of this book, research papers seemed like a monsters that needed to be slain. Now you can see that the monster metaphor isn't particularly accurate—writing a paper isn't some herculean task, it is a series of manageable steps that you are fully capable of completing.

As with any skill, writing research papers won't suddenly become easy for you overnight. Writing takes practice, and everyone messes up along the way. Some students find that the writing process comes easily once they learn the basics. Others struggle with developing a style or constructing a strong, logical argument. Even students who are naturally talented make mistakes, because they simply haven't written a research paper before. Like learning an instrument or playing a sport, you will get better at writing a research paper every time you do it.

This book presented 101 tips to help you write your research paper and make your work stand out. Of these tips, I argue that Tip #6 is by far the most important. From Chapter 1:

> # Tip · #6 ¶ ▶
>
> While · you · are · working · on · your · research · paper, · try · to · find · time · to · ask · your · teacher · questions · if · you · encounter · problems · along · the · way. · Some · students · think · that · asking · many · questions · makes · them · seem · stupid. · In · reality, · it · shows · your · teacher · or · instructor · that · you · care · about · succeeding. ¶

No matter your skill level as a writer and researcher, knowing how to ask for help is perhaps the most important skill of all. Even if you are an experienced writer, you will someday encounter a paper topic that stumps you, or a teacher who has different requirements than what you expect.

Many students who have written research papers in high school panic when they get to college and must cite their sources in Turabian instead of MLA. Others successfully write their first paper, only to freak out when they receive a grade that is not at the level they are used to. If you struggle — whether you are writing your first research paper or your tenth — it doesn't mean you should panic. It doesn't mean that writing isn't in your future, or that your class is too hard. It means that you are facing a task which you haven't faced before. Think back to the skills you have acquired, and ask about the issues that still stump you.

You might be wondering what the point of writing research papers is in the long-term—most adults don't write research papers for their day jobs. Unless you want to be a writer or an academic, you might not have to write a full-length research paper after you have finished school, but the skills you acquire from writing research papers carry over into nearly any field. Knowing how to craft an argument and persuade your reader will help you no matter what your career is. Writing and research skills—knowing how to determine which information is reliable and find answers to your questions—are likewise essential, especially with the unfortunate prevalence of misinformation on the Internet. And even if you go into a career where all the skills you've learned from research papers seem irrelevant, learning to persevere when something is difficult will help you no matter what career you chose. So even if you know that writing research papers is not something you want to do in your future, the skills you will acquire will serve you well no matter where life takes you.

Author's Note

I wrote my first research paper when I was in seventh grade. It was about the Manhattan Project and the development of the first atomic bomb. I was a pretty enthusiastic middle-schooler, and I remember staying up late over Thanksgiving break reading long academic books. By the time I wrote, revised, and turned in that paper, I thought it was basically the best paper in the world.

I don't go back and read that paper very often because it makes me cringe. (It is nowhere near the best paper in the world). Since then, I've written a lot of research papers, most of which have been much better. I've written a lot about history — topics ranging from apartheid in South Africa to American railroads in the 1870s — and about literature. One of my favorite papers I've ever written analyzed the choreopoem "For colored girls who have considered suicide / when the rainbow is enuf," by Ntozake Shange. I've written some papers for science classes, a few in economics, one in math, and a few entirely in Spanish, which is not my first language.

While all of the papers I have written are very different from one another, they still follow the same basic principles. They all had thesis statements and brought in evidence to support my argument. I have little doubt that writing each of them made me a stronger writer and student. The skills I learned researching novels and authors for an English literature class still applied when I was studying literature in Spanish. The ability to read primary sources that I gained when I was writing about the atomic bomb in seventh grade helped me write better history papers later on. The science papers I wrote in high school helped me analyze data for the economics papers I wrote in college, and the math paper I had to write taught me how to persevere through really tough assignments. In a lot of ways, writing research papers opened up a whole field of opportunities for me. For example, I never would have started writing books if I hadn't written many papers first.

As a college student, I'm much more versed in researching and writing than I was in seventh grade—and I'm also much better at recognizing my own limitations. Like any writer, I make plenty of mistakes. I've turned in papers with typos and lost points for it; life went on. I've picked paper topics only to realize they were incredibly boring; I've had to modify my thesis statement at the last minute when I encountered new evidence. I can tell you from personal experience that, no matter how easy a paper seems, trying to write it the night before is never, ever a good idea.

Despite some difficulties over the years, I can say with certainty that writing research papers does get easier. The more you read and learn and write, the more naturally these tasks will come. Don't be afraid to make mistakes. Don't be afraid to get insanely excited about a nerdy topic—someday, your ability to spew weird trivia facts will come in handy. Don't be afraid to work hard, and don't be afraid to ask for help when working hard isn't enough.

No matter your previous experiences or capabilities, writing a research paper shouldn't be a terribly painful experience. It should be something you learn from. So as you join the ranks of people who have written research papers, be proud of what you've accomplished, and be ready to keep improving. That's all you can ask of yourself.

Glossary

active voice: A sentence where the subject of the sentence completes the action described by the verb. For example: "The dog chased after the ball."

adjective: a word which describes a noun. For example: blue, seven, tall, pretty, lucky.

adverb: a word which describes a verb, adjective, or another adverb. For example: quickly, very, often, happily.

alignment: the way text is set up on a page. For a research paper, you will want your text to be aligned left.

anecdote: A short story describing an event.

anonymous source: A source with an unknown author.

audience: In the context of a research paper, the intended reader or readers.

bias: The tendency of an author or source to promote an opinion or point of view.

bibliography: A list of sources that were used for research, included at the end of a research paper.

brainstorming: Generating ideas and drawing informal connections based on previous knowledge or research.

cherry-picking: Selecting only certain facts (and omitting other ones) to make a certain point.

chronology: A listing of events in the order that they occurred.

clause: A phrase with a subject and a verb.

comma splice: A grammatical error where two independent clauses are connected by a comma.

complex sentence: A sentence containing one independent and one dependent clause.

complex-compound sentence: A sentence containing two independent clauses connected by a coordinating conjunction and a dependent clause with a subordinating conjunction.

compound sentence: A sentence containing two independent clauses connected by a coordinating conjunction.

coordinating conjunction: A conjunction connecting two independents clauses. Coordinating conjunctions can be remembered with the acronym FANBOYS: for, and, no, but, or, yet and so.

correlation: A relationship between two variables or events.

credentials: Qualifications, such as degrees or relevant experience, that give an author credibility.

dash: A punctuation mark used to break up words or phrases.

dependent clause: A clause beginning with a subordinating conjunction.

editing: Making change changes to your paper, such as word choice and sentence structure.

endnote: A form of inline citation that indicates the source for a quote, fact, or idea using a number in the text, which matches with a number included at the end of the paper.

fact-checking: Using multiple sources to verify information.

footnote: A form of inline citation that indicates the source for a quote, fact, or idea using a number in the text, which matches with a number included at the bottom of the page.

font: the standard appearance of type. For your research paper, you want to use a professional-looking font, such as Times New Roman.

footer: the whitespace at the bottom of the page. For a research paper, you should allow at least one inch for a footer, although you may put a page number in that space.

fragment: A phrase intended a sentence that does not contain a full subject, verb, and complete thought.

freewriting: A form of brainstorming where you write all your ideas about a topic or question, without worrying about spelling, grammar, order, or other considerations.

header: the whitespace at the top of the page. For a research paper, you should allow at least one inch for a header, although you may put a page number in that space.

homophone: A pair of words that sound alike but are spelled differently and have different meanings.

hook: An alluring or exciting opening sentence designed to draw in your reader and make them want to read more.

hyphen: A punctuation mark used to bring together two words.

independent clause: A phrase with a subject, verb, and complete thought which could stand alone as its own sentence.

inline citations: Footnotes, endnotes, or parentheticals which indicate the source of a fact or idea in a research paper.

inverted pyramid: A shape—which also resembles an upside-down triangle—which demonstrates the ideal structure for an introduction: starting out broad and narrowing.

margin: the whitespace around the edges of the paper. For a research paper, you should typically use one-inch margins.

microfilm: Film—often available at libraries—that has a photographic copy of old documents, such as newspapers.

mind-mapping: A brainstorming technique where you visually draw out connections between topics, using circles and lines.

misquoting: Incorrectly quoting a source—you should never do this in your paper!

noun: a word or phrase representing a person, place, or thing. For example: dog, White House, brother, dingo.

outlining: Drafting a condensed, bullet-point version of your paper that shows the main ideas and the order they go in.

paraphrase: Rewriting someone else's ideas in your own words.

parenthetical citation: A form of inline citation that indicates the source for a quote, fact, or idea using parentheses (usually with the author's name and a page number) in the text.

passive voice: A sentence where verb acts upon the subject of the sentence, and the person or thing that completes the action is omitted or described via a preposition phrase. For example: "The ball was chased after by the dog."

peer-reviewed journal articles: Academic papers that—in addition to being written by a strong researcher—have been examined by other experts in the field to ensure accuracy.

plagiarism: A form of cheating based on using someone else's words or ideas without giving them credit.

primary source: A firsthand account of information without any analysis or interpretation.

research: Investigation or information-gathering about a subject.

revising: Reading your paper after you have a complete draft and making necessary changes to its content and structure.

rhetorical question: A question asked without an expected answer. Questions in research papers are almost always rhetorical—while the writer may be hoping to force the reader to think, the reader does not actually answer the question.

run-on sentence: A grammatically incorrect sentence that occurs when two independent clauses are connected improperly.

secondary source: A source written by researchers based on primary sources, and other secondary sources.

simple sentence: A sentence made up of a single clause.

size: with reference to fonts, the height and width of characters. For your research paper, you should typically use 12-point font.

spacing: with reference to research papers, the amount of whitespace between lines. You should typically double-space your research paper.

subordinating conjunction: A word that introduces a dependent clause. For example: after, although, because and since.

summarize: Explaining someone else's ideas in a shorter, condensed version.

tertiary sources: Encyclopedias, dictionaries, atlases, or other reference books used for background research.

thesis statement: A sentence or two in the introduction which state the main argument of your paper.

tone: The attitude of the writer toward the reader, conveyed by the language and word choices in a paper.

verb: a word expressing an action, occurrence, or state of being. For example: run, jump, be, grow, seem.

works cited: A list of sources that contributed specific facts or information, included at the end of a research paper.

Bibliography

"Americans with Criminal Records." *The Sentencing Project*. 2015. Web. **http://www.sentencingproject.org/wp-content/uploads/2015/11/ Americans-with-Criminal-Records-Poverty-and-Opportunity -Profile.pdf**. Accessed 25 Nov. 2016.

Fesler, J. W. "Lincoln's Gettysburg Address." *Indiana Magazine of History* 40.3 (1944): 209-26. Web. Accessed 25 Nov. 2016.

Katula, Richard A. "The Gettysburg Address as the Centerpiece of American Racial Discourse." *The Journal of Blacks in Higher Education* 28 (2000): 110-11. Web. Accessed 25 Nov. 2016.

Keeling, M. J., and C. A. Gilligan. "Bubonic Plague: A Metapopulation Model of a Zoonosis." *Proceedings: Biological Sciences* 267, no. 1458 (2000): 2219-230. **http://www.jstor.org/stable/2665900**. Accessed 25 Nov. 2016.

Keyes, Ralph. "Ask Not Where This Quote Came From." *Washington Post*. 4 Jun. 2006. Web. **http://www.washingtonpost.com/wp-dyn/content/ article/2006/06/02/AR2006060201406.html**. Accessed 25 Nov. 2016.

Kristof, Nicholas. "Smart Guns Save Lives. So Where Are They?" *New York Times*. 17 Jan. 2015. Web. **http://www.nytimes.com/2015/01/18/**

opinion/sunday/nicholas-kristof-smart-guns-save-lives-so-where
-are-they.html. Accessed 25 Nov. 2016.

Lincoln, Abraham. "The Gettysburg Address." 19 Nov. 1863. Web. http://
www.d.umn.edu/~rmaclin/gettysburg-address.html. Accessed 25
Nov. 2016.

Lombrozo, Tania. "This Could Have Been Shorter." *National Public Radio*. 3 Feb. 2014. http://www.npr.org/sections/13.7/2014/02/03/
270680304/this-could-have-been-shorter. Accessed 1 Jan. 2017.

Mulisch, Harry. *The Assault*. Translated by Claire Nicholas White. New
York: Pantheon Books, 1985.

"Plagiarism." *Merriam-Webster Dictionary*. No date. Web. http://www
.merriam-webster.com/dictionary/plagiarism. Accessed 25 Nov.
2016.

Phillips, Tom. "Nobel author Gabriel García Márquez wins 17-year legal fight over murder classic." *The Guardian*. 30 Nov. 2011. Web.
https://www.theguardian.com/books/2011/nov/30/gabriel-garcia
-marquez-court-victory. Accessed 25 Nov. 2016.

Sapolsky, Robert M. "The Spirit of the 1914 Christmas Truce." *The Wall
Street Journal*. 19 Dec 2014. Web. http://www.wsj.com/articles/the
-spirit-of-the-1914-christmas-truce-1419006906. Accessed 25 Nov.
2016.

Sullivan, Edward T. *The Ultimate Weapon: The Race to Develop the Atomic
Bomb*. New York: Holiday House, 2007.

World Bank. 2016. *Poverty and Shared Prosperity 2016: Taking on Inequality*. Washington, DC: World Bank. Web. https://openknowledge
.worldbank.org/bitstream/handle/10986/25078/9781464809583
.pdf. Accessed 25 Nov. 2016.

Index

About the Author

Jessica E. Piper is an American writer. She grew up in Colorado before moving to Maine for college, and she has written a lot of research papers over the years. Some of her favorite writing topics include obscure historical happenings, contemporary social issues, and analysis of popular culture. She currently studies economics and works for a weekly college newspaper. When she is not writing, she enjoys music, travel, and spending time with friends and family.